BEST
IN
CLASS

LYNNE BREIL

ETIQUETTE and PEOPLE SKILLS FOR YOUR CAREER

Kendall Hunt
publishing company

Kendall Hunt
publishing company

www.kendallhunt.com
Send all inquiries to:
4050 Westmark Drive
Dubuque, IA 52004-1840

Published in the United States of America

CONTENTS

CHAPTER 1 FIRST IMPRESSIONS AND PROFESSIONAL PRESENCE 1

CHAPTER 2 TECHNOLOGY ETIQUETTE 66

CHAPTER 3 GENERAL WORKPLACE ETIQUETTE 92

CHAPTER 4 BUSINESS SOCIAL EVENTS AND THE BUSINESS MEAL 110

CHAPTER 5 GOING GLOBAL 160

PREFACE

There's a hilarious clip known as <u>The Bobs,</u> from the 1999 American comedy film, **Office Space.** In this 1-minute clip, 2 consultants are interviewing an employee to determine the value of his job and whether he will keep his job after a major downsizing.

The employee appears nervous and uncomfortable when asked what he does in his position as the consultants continue to ask pointed questions. Finally, his patience (and self-control) disappear and in an enraged voice he says, "I deal with the %!@# customer so the engineers don't have to! I have **people skills!** I am good at dealing with people! What the %!@# is wrong with you people?"

This short clip shows a comical, yet obviously inaccurate portrayal of **people skills.** It's the exact opposite of the what **people skills** really are, and the consultants in the movie know it. Truth is, **people skills** are characteristic of those who *get*, *keep*, and *move up* in their jobs.

Learning about **etiquette** and **people skills** doesn't mean you need to change who you are, it means becoming more aware of your behaviors so you can enhance a natural strength or modify one that may be creating a distraction.

Bringing civility back into the workplace is not a lost cause, especially in this era of e-communication. Observing manners at work will impress your boss, build relationships with decision-makers in your industry, and smooth the way with your competitors. Classy, kind, considerate, and smart people are the ones who get ahead.

Whether you're planning to open a car restoration business like my student, Sam, or work for a non-profit like Bella, this book will help you build your personal brand with etiquette and people skills.

ACKNOWLEDGMENTS

I'm so pleased to present this book to readers who know that behaving in business was, is, and always will be important. I've researched and listened to people comment on **Business Etiquette** for a quarter of a century.

First and foremost, I'd like to thank my husband, John Breil. You're the "someone to watch over me." You gave me space to write, took over business projects when I was on a deadline, updated information for this book, and brewed the coffee. You also gave me feedback that I didn't want to hear because I don't ever think I'm wrong. (My biggest flaw!) You've added so much to this project by sharing your expertise and providing data to support the information. Thank you and I love you.

I'd also like to thank my *millennial* sons, James Tully and Patrick Tully, who supported me in this project and were the sources of several examples told within. Each of you have outstanding "people skills" and you know it. Those skills, and your work ethic, have without question helped to position you as a television news anchor (James) and a chief technology officer (Patrick) so early in your careers. I'm very proud of the two of you for your accomplishments. Thanks for sharing your stories with me for this book. I hope you'll be ready to help with the next one!

I'm grateful to my colleagues—in particular, Carol Kivler, Karen Lawson, and Marjorie Brody (speakers and consultants in their own right)—who've motivated me to finish this book. You all lead by example and you're all amazing.

To my associate, Christina Butler Haubert—you've got the right combination of experience, presence, and "smarts" to continue to spread the gospel about etiquette in business. Just go do it. I'll always be here to help.

A word of thanks to clients Allison Venella (Villanova University), Beth Brennan (Penn State University–York), Patricia Jepsen (Penn State University–Berks), Dean George Ebbs and the Luter School of Business (Christopher Newport University), and the Phi Alpha Delta Law Fraternity (Widener School of Law–Delaware). Working with each of you gave me the incentive to write this book.

I owe a debt of gratitude to my clients who let me beg, borrow, and steal their examples for this publication. (Names were withheld to protect the guilty.) I've had input from senior executives, hiring managers, human resource professionals, and training specialists. I'll always be grateful for the opportunities our valued clients have given me.

I'm deeply appreciative to York College Graham School of Business colleagues, and my dear personal friends, Dr. David Greisler and Professor Christopher Meisenhelter, who decided years ago that business and communication go together. And then they invited me to help with a business department project and it was the start of something big. I admire and respect you both, and I couldn't have done this book without your support and encouragement.

Last but not least, to my students (past and present) at York College of Pennsylvania and to Dr. Brian Furio (York College Department of Communication and the Arts) who hired me twenty-seven years ago. You gave me that very first opportunity to use the classroom as a venue to share the topic of business etiquette, and give our students The Professional Edge. Who would have guessed what that opportunity would bring?

ABOUT THE AUTHOR

Lynne Breil, CSP is the CEO and founder of The Professional Edge, Inc. She is a sought-after speaker on the topics of business etiquette, presentation skills, and leadership presence. The *Philadelphia Inquirer* dubbed her "The Manners Maven," and she has spoken to audiences across the country and internationally on "People Skills" in the workplace.

Her teaching experience includes over twenty-five years at the college level. Currently she is an adjunct professor of business communications at York College of Pennsylvania.

Lynne has been an active leader in the central Pennsylvania business community having led the Women's Business Center Organization and been a member of the York, Lancaster, and Harrisburg (Pennsylvania) chambers of commerce. She has also been recognized as one of Pennsylvania's Best 50 Women in Business.

A recipient of the Certified Speaking Professional designation from the National Speakers Association and the International Federation for Professional Speakers, Lynne is recognized by her peers for excellence in professional and platform skills in the speaking industry. She is a trained concert pianist and was—almost seven dog years ago—a semi-finalist in the Miss America pageant.

Lynne is also the author of the pocket guide: <u>Share a Meal. Close a Deal.</u> *<u>Business Dining from A-Z.</u>*

John R. Breil

John Breil is a guy with a well-worn passport and the international business experience and insight to provide sought-after management coaching. John specializes in leadership and executive coaching across cultures and works with managers and supervisors in a variety of industries including: manufacturing, finance, healthcare, and non-profit. He has coined the phrase, "You have A-L-O-T (Always Listen Observe and Think) when going Global."

Christina Butler

Christina Butler has covered breaking news, natural disasters, and all levels of politics as a television news veteran of 15 years. In television, she's worked nearly every position in the newsroom from assignment manager to anchor. As a speaker, she uses her expertise in impression management, relationship building, and media consulting to help her clients in a variety of industries. Christina is also an Emmy nominated news reporter and a popular speaker on the topics of business etiquette, professional presence, and media management.

First Impressions and Professional Presence

INTRODUCTION: IT'S WHAT'S UP FRONT THAT COUNTS

How do you want people to see you as a professional? What adjectives would you like your prospective boss or future coworkers to use to describe you? This is a question I ask to start many of my programs on business etiquette and professional presence. Many answers are similar: *knowledgeable, hardworking, trustworthy, friendly, responsive, competent, approachable, creative, problem-solver...* and many more.

Choose three words for yourself and let them be *your* criteria for everything you do in business. That includes how you act, how you look, and what you say.

Chances are, you're not going to get every job you interview for or "win" every proposal you present to a client. This chapter will give you a solid start in understanding and creating a powerful and positive first impression in business, when it counts the most.

FIRST IMPRESSIONS IN BUSINESS

Will Rogers said it best. Wouldn't it be great if people could withhold their first impressions until they got to know the *real* you, then make a judgment? It's what's inside that counts, right? It doesn't work that way, unfortunately. In her book *EP Executive Presence*, Sylvia Hewlett cites research from the Harvard Medical School which suggests that colleagues size up your competence in 250 milliseconds, based on your appearance alone.

Psychologists say that 60 to 80 percent of your message is communicated through nonverbal signals, but we rarely pay attention to what we are doing with our bodies and our voice and how those influence our intended message. When you're face to face with someone, you have three communication forces working either for you or against you: how you look (visual signals), how you sound (vocal signals), and what you say (verbal signals). These three communication signals are important in other cultures, too, but vary in their interpretation (which we will share in Chapter 5's "Business Etiquette Abroad").

Now that you know a first impression can last less than a second, here are the things people notice when you meet them for the first time, and what you can do to maximize your first impression in a professional setting:

Your first words: Use a form of "thanks." There are dozens of ways you can do this, for example: *"Thanks for taking the time to meet me today"* ... *"Thanks for squeezing me into your schedule"* ... *"Thanks for arranging this meeting"* ... *"Thanks for giving me information on where to park"* ... *"Thanks for bringing in your team to talk with us"* ... and so forth.

Your first steps: Move with purpose and pick up your pace. People can—and will—judge your mood by your movements, and those who move more quickly are perceived as those who get more done. When you're entering a room, an office building, or an area where you'll be meeting others for the first time, consider how you move. From your first step, pay attention to your posture, your eye contact (look straight ahead, not down to the floor), and your stride.

Your first twelve inches: Imagine a twelve-inch box from the top of your head to your shoulders. This area stands out when others meet you for the first time, so pay attention to what is in the "imaginary" box.

For women, your hairstyle, jewelry, accessories (eyeglasses are a *power* accessory for women), makeup, and neckline are important. For men, your hairstyle, beard/shaving detail, collar (undershirts should <u>not</u> be visible), how your necktie is tied, are all important. Our associate, Christina Butler, who has worked as a television news reporter says this 12-inch box is critical when a reporter is first seen on camera.

Photo taken by Lynne Breil.

Your last twelve inches: The floor to midcalf are also among the first places people look to get a sense of how much you pay attention to detail. The condition and cleanliness of your shoes, soles, toes (ladies, if you're wearing open-toed shoes, get or give yourself a pedicure), socks, hosiery, and length of slacks or trousers all need attention. Guys, match your socks to your shoes and make sure they're long enough to cover your skin when crossing your legs. Ladies, wear hosiery with dresses or skirts for important business meetings (too much skin with a short skirt is not appropriate), select shoes that don't make noise when you walk, and cross your legs properly.

GREETINGS, INTRODUCTIONS, AND HANDSHAKES

"A good beginning makes a good ending."
—ENGLISH PROVERB

© fizkes/Shutterstock.com

In business, you shake a lot of hands. What does your handshake say about you? It's worth considering, because in the American business culture, you will be judged by the way you shake hands with someone. Though it might not seem fair or accurate (it's not) we still perceive others, and judge their personality traits, by how they shake hands.

A limp handshake is often interpreted as showing a lack of confidence or weakness. A "bone crusher" handshake is often taken as being aggressive, a power player, or overconfident.

Three steps to a powerful handshake when you are meeting someone are:

1. Extend your hand as you say your name.
2. Keep your hand vertical (up and down), with your thumb joint open, and touch the other person's hand, interlinking at the web (the part between your thumb and index finger); close your hand around the other person's palm.
3. Give two to three firm shakes, from the elbow (not the shoulder). Do not grasp the person's hand with your other hand (the two-handed shake), especially if it's a first meeting. The two-handed handshake can be perceived as being "too familiar."

WHEN TO SHAKE HANDS

Many young professionals aren't sure whether they should *initiate* a handshake with a senior-ranking person. First, congratulations on taking the initiative if you approach that person first. Go ahead and extend your hand if the senior person doesn't extend his or hers. Think of handshakes as in the Wild West *luck of the draw*. Whomever shakes first has the upper hand.

In business, regardless of gender, it doesn't matter who initiates the handshake as it used to many years ago. If a man appears to be hesitant to extend his hand to shake hands, a woman can simplify this by extending her hand. Handshakes are important as part of a business greeting, and they're the *only legitimate form of touching in business*.

What about the "sticky" situations you can encounter when shaking hands? Here are a few examples and how to handle them.

Sneezing and the common cold. Apologize upfront if you have a cold and do not want to shake hands. Others will understand, and they'll thank you.

The "no shake." When someone does respond to your extended hand with a handshake, just withdraw your hand and continue with conversation. Either the person is very shy or his or her religious affiliation may prohibit touching other people, even in business situations.

The "sweaty palmer." Some people have a natural tendency to get sweaty hands. If that's **you**, dry your hands on a piece of clothing before shaking.

The "hand holder." After three shakes, your natural instincts will probably tell you the handshake is over, but some people want to linger on. In this case, release your grip and <u>do not regrip</u>, which may signal to the hand holder that you're starting over again.

When you should shake hands:

- During introductions and farewells (e.g., at the beginning and end of a job interview).
- When greeting someone from outside your organization (e.g., campus visitors, vendors, visiting professors, new students at a formal orientation meeting).
- When you formalize an agreement (e.g., accepting a job or internship face to face and the terms of that employment).
- When you run into a professional business acquaintance you haven't seen for a while.

INTRODUCING...YOU!

In some business situations, you'll be on your own to introduce yourself to others in the room. It's scary when you don't know anyone, but you have the choice to either sit by yourself or move around the room and meet others.

Several years ago, I spoke at an on-campus event with industry professionals from engineering firms. Senior engineering major students were invited to attend. When I arrived during the "mix and mingle" hour, the students had taken their seats together at the same table, awaiting dinner. The industry professionals were doing what you'd expect them to be doing—working the room. I walked over to the students and asked them if they were aware that almost any of the professionals in the room (all movers and shakers in the engineering industry) could potentially hire them. I then told them that this is probably the best opportunity for them to get up out of their seats and start to meet people who could influence their careers. At first, I got some unwelcome stares. Eventually, the students *did* get up out of their chairs, and though they were quite uncomfortable, they approached the industry professionals. Maybe it was the most uncomfortable moment in their semester, but it was also the biggest opportunity for them.

When you meet someone at an event who asks you what you do, have a one-sentence **networking introduction** ready. There will be many events—from career fairs to alumni dinners—where you'll get this opportunity. Remember the point of a networking introduction is not to "sell yourself" but to spark conversation with someone, leading to further conversation. We'll talk more about the networking event later.

Here are a few tips:

- Say who you are. *"I'm a supply chain major at ABC University."*
- Say who you want to work for. *"I'd like to work for a manufacturer with a global presence."*
- Say how you can help this organization. *"I analyze data to improve project timelines."*

Once you've answered these three questions, put the information together into one sentence, which is your networking introduction:

"I'm a supply chain major who can analyze data for project management in global manufacturing."

Maybe you modify your ten-second introduction depending on where you are, tailoring it to the situation. You might use a slightly different introduction when meeting a recruiter at a career fair. After you make your introduction, your contact might ask you a question, so be prepared to listen so you know how to respond.

It pays to take time to craft your ten-second networking introduction so that you feel prepared and confident.

INTRODUCING OTHERS

When you introduce others in business, it's a moment of truth. People form an impression of your social savvy and how you handle a situation where people can feel left out unless you include them in the introduction.

Business introductions have three parts:

1. First, **say the name of the "most important" person first**. (Gender or age is not a determining factor; opt for the senior-ranking person or the client.)
2. **Say the first and last name of each person.** *"James Wilson, this is Brian Jones."*
3. **Say something about the persons being introduced**. *"James Wilson, this is Brian Jones, our account representative. Brian, James is our new client from XYZ Corporation."*

If you don't know who the most important person is in an introduction, default to social rules which would dictate that you start with the *older* person or the *female*. If you forget the name of the person you're about to introduce, be upfront and apologize by saying, "I'm sorry, could you please tell me your name again?" Everyone does it, and by admitting you've forgotten the name and offering an apology, you're making the person feel important, not offended. If no one introduces you at an event, introduce yourself. Smile and say, "Hi, I'm Lynne Breil. I don't think we've met."

Introducing others is an important business practice, but don't be too hard on yourself if you make a mistake in an introduction. Remember that a "botched up" introduction is better than none at all.

PROFESSIONAL ATTIRE AND GROOMING

"How you look tells the world how you feel."
—SERGIO VALENTE, ITALIAN FASHION DESIGNER

© Josep Suria/Shutterstock.com

ESTABLISH A DRESS CODE FOR YOURSELF

Look at people at the top of organizations. Observe those people who are leading or influencing others. What are they wearing? Is it trendy or conservative? The answer to a lot of your "what I should wear to work?" questions will be answered when you observe the leaders in your organization or in other similar organizations. What do your "leaders" wear on business casual day? What do they wear to client meetings or even client outings?

One semester, a student approached me after class and confessed that she really "needed to go shopping" after hearing that I requested all students to dress in business professional attire for their speeches. In her part-time job decorating cakes at a grocery store bakery and as a student, her standard attire of sweats and t-shirts pretty much summed up her wardrobe. She had some money saved to buy more professional attire but wasn't exactly sure what to buy.

As a new professional, you may be just starting to build a business wardrobe. Every piece you buy should meet the following criteria:

- **Image.** What professional image would you like to project? (Refer back to the question I asked at the beginning of this chapter about how you want to be perceived as a professional.)
- **Message.** What conveys good judgment and says to others that you want to be taken seriously? What pieces, colors, fabrics, and accessories make you feel your best when you're "on task"? What were you wearing when you received compliments *in a professional setting*?
- **Fit.** What items fit you appropriately and do not call attention to areas you *don't* want to emphasize? (Remember: anything you wear that emphasizes the biological differences between a man and a woman is not appropriate for most business or workplace settings.)

Once you can answer these questions, you can establish a professional style and you can shop more smartly by selecting items that are appropriate in your industry and make you feel and look good.

A few years ago, I was hired to take a client shopping to help her select (and purchase—she had a budget) some items for her business wardrobe. Her boss told me she was sending my client to a conference where she would have a highly visible role and be interacting with attendees from around the country. She wanted my client to make a good impression. Her existing business wardrobe was, in her boss's opinion, not appropriate. Here was a company (and a supervisor) willing to make an investment to help an individual make a positive impression in what she was wearing so that it underscored her professional skills rather than detracted from them.

To prepare for our first shopping trip, I did some advance work as I usually do, to preselect some items for my client. I based my selection on her favorite colors, her body type and height, her industry and job responsibilities, and her age. I couldn't wait to show her the things I set aside!

It took some time, but she finally accepted the fact that she was buying the wrong size (too small) and the wrong styles (too adolescent). When she understood that buying "trendy" is *not* an investment and considered the *"cost per wearing"* of each item, she adapted a new approach to investing in clothes for work. She was pleased when we selected a color palette that worked for her, and a manufacturer that produced a quality garment which fit her well and was appropriate for a business environment. Plus, she felt good in the clothes and accessories we selected.

Even without a consultant helping you select your business wardrobe, dressing appropriately for work can put a dent in your budget. There are ways to stretch a dollar in business dress, and the information below will help you consider your purchases an *investment* rather than a liability.

How Much Should You Spend?

The best way to spend wisely is to know what you're looking for. Quality rather than quantity is the standard when building a professional wardrobe. Technically, clothing is not an investment because clothes do not appreciate. They're clothes. But if you think of your business wardrobe as *appreciative* (something that *appreciates*), then you and your colleagues can and will *appreciate* the way you look.

Buy the best that you can sensibly afford and you will get your money's worth. To determine the actual cost of an outfit, use this formula:

$$\frac{\text{Cost}}{\text{Total number of wearings*}} = \textbf{Cost per wearing}$$

* _____ wearings per month X _____ months worn X _____ years worn = Total # of wearings

I'll give you two examples. My older son, who is a television news anchor, recently purchased several new suits, with the help of the station's image consultant. The suits he purchased were around $225 each, on sale.

The suits were good quality, wool-blend suits that can be worn year-round. On an average, he wears each of them three or four times a month. They are conservatively styled, tailored to fit, and in traditional colors of blues, greys, charcoals, and black. He figures he will wear them for about three years. As an aside, his image consultant told him that in TV news the only acceptable shirt colors for men are white and light blue. *Guys—when in doubt, always wear a white or light blue shirt.* My son could start a men's section in a department store with his shirt wardrobe!

Let's do some math. A $225 suit, worn four times a month for three years and which can be worn for twelve months yields 144 wearings; $225 divided by 144 equals $1.56 per wearing.

Compare that investment with one a colleague of mine made recently at a chic consignment shop in Washington, D.C. She was seduced by the designer label, and though the suit wasn't the best fit, she figured getting it tailored would be worth the investment. (She later admitted that the suit had a somewhat trendy style and was more evening appropriate than daytime appropriate.) She paid $50 for the suit and $110 for the tailoring, for a total of $160. The suit is appropriate for year-round wear, but she's worn it only four months per year, once a month, for two years; a total of eight wearings. Thus, $160 divided by 8 equals $20 per wearing.

Which was the better investment? The $225 suit with a cost per wearing of $1.56 or a $50 designer suit with a $110 tailoring price tag and a cost per wearing of $20? Factor in dry cleaning costs and the $225 suit still makes more sense.

Investing in your workplace attire is not only a wise decision but also a way to convey a quality image. Trust me, you won't get tired of your clothes when you *invest* in them.

CLOTHES ENCOUNTERS: WHAT **NOT** TO WEAR TO WORK

There are jobs where the exception (such as visible tattoos, assorted body piercings, and blue hair) is the norm. And then there are jobs where uniforms dictate what you wear, and your employer determines how they are to be worn. And yes, it *is* legal for employers to set guidelines for how they want you to dress when you're on the job.

For much of the rest of us who work in other environments, we have freedom of choice ... sort of. My students at York College of Pennsylvania understand why I suggest they dress more conservatively than trendy when representing the college in the business community whether off campus or on campus. Occasionally I have a student who offers a mild protest, claiming that *unconventional* is "his or her" style and they want to "stand out." While I applaud individual style, in a professional setting your *unconventional* style could take away from your other assets, and work against you.

An article published in the *Psychology of Women Quarterly* (a scholarly journal put out by the American Psychological Association) claimed that although physical attractiveness is generally an advantage in the workplace, "a sexy self-presentation harms businesswomen" who are in, or who aspire to, managerial-level jobs. Data supports that more conservative dress is "risk free" and does not interfere with but rather supports how people perceive your capabilities in a positive way. You can turn on TV and find that "sex sells," even in the news. But for many professionals who are judging you, remember that sexuality scrambles the mind. It's distracting and confusing.

I'll never forget one of the participants in a program I presented recently. The setting was a corporate-wide sales meeting, and the participants (all sales professionals) were told that "business casual dress" was the code of dress for the meetings. I entered the training room and my eyes went right to one of the participants: a guy with the biggest "guns" (biceps) I've ever seen! His polo shirt was stretched at the sleeves to accommodate his oversized muscles. My eyes kept going to this "vision" for most of the day, and it was distracting to say the least. Imagine if he were in front of a group of clients making a sales pitch or giving information. They would likely remember little else than his biceps, like I did.

For both sexes, what constitutes acceptable dress can vary from one company to another. Some industries and some parts of the country may be more casual and trendy than others. In any case, make your decision based on what you see most people who work in that organization wear. If you're an intern, observe. If you don't know what's acceptable regarding attire and grooming, ask someone from human resources, a trusted coworker, or your supervisor.

You can always use this criteria: "If I were to have an unexpected meeting with a chief executive, could I go dressed in what I'm wearing?"

Erring on the side of too trendy or too casual could be a big mistake. Just remember: You'll never go wrong by dressing conservatively.

Following is a baseline list of **what not to wear to work.** It is a list I've compiled from talking to client groups and audiences and gathering current online research.

- **Anything see-through or sheer:** T-shirts, see-through blouses, and transparent skirts or dresses are not right for a professional setting. Save them for the weekend or nonwork events. For lighter fabrics, a camisole or undershirt should always be worn.
- **Yoga pants and leggings:** This item is up for contention between younger and older employees. Gen Xers (born 1965–1976) and Baby Boomers (born 1946–1964) say "no," Millennials (born 1977–1995) and Gen Z'ers (also known as Centennials, born 1996–on) say "okay." My advice is to follow what your bosses or higher ranking individuals are wearing—if they're not wearing leggings, you shouldn't either.
- **Anything too tight, too short, or too baggy:** You're not a rapper from the mid-2000s, so don't dress like one. As I've stated before, clothes that are too tight or emphasize biological differences between males and females are also a major no-no.
- **Cold shoulder tops, halter tops, or tank tops:** These are not appropriate for the office. As a female, I do not wear sleeveless tops or sleeveless dresses in conservative business settings or when I'm giving a presentation. Men should always keep their upper arms clothed at work. Tank tops or halter tops can be layered under a blazer or sweater.
- **Anything that shows off your cleavage, back, or tummy:** The more skin you show, the less influence you have. Keep your torso and back covered in the workplace. A student once asked me how much cleavage is appropriate for the workplace. And she was serious! Another time, I switched tops with a student who was about to present to a group of executives because her midriff was exposed. I kept my blazer on, wearing her top while she presented in more appropriate attire. Think what you want to draw attention to when you're at work or in front of others.

- **Visible undergarments:** Neither gender should show underwear, but they *should* wear underwear. Low-rise jeans with boxers or undies peeking out, or visible bra straps are for another time and not at work.
- **A lot of animal print:** I like animal print, and it's been a timeless fashion statement for women. But, you don't want to be known as "the person with leopard-print pants." Animal prints are fine as an accessory, but probably overdone if you're wearing them "head to toe."
- **Pajamas:** This includes those flannel drawstring sleep pants and fleece tops that are so comfy to slip into after work. It looks like you're about to take a nap or that you simply "rolled out of bed" before coming to work, which is probably true.
- **Crocs:** Some are high fashion (still not appropriate), and some are functional (if you're in the food preparation industry). For the rest of us, they're a "no" for the workplace. Plus, I'm told by one young professional that Crocs make your feet smell bad.
- **Anything you would wear to the gym:** Workout clothes aren't for the workplace. That includes hoodies and that nylon, sweat-wicking, breathable, and super-stretchy t-shirt you received when you ran the 5K turkey trot last Thanksgiving.
- **Baseball hats, bandanas, or head wraps:** Baseball caps are not appropriate for wearing indoors, at your job or internship. Although head wraps are an article of cultural pride, you may have to contend with stares, uninvited comments, and potential criticisms from coworkers and higher-ups.
- **Anything you bought for clubbing or bar-hopping:** You can experiment with these by converting them from day to night with a blazer or cardigan. Otherwise, save for them for the weekend.
- **Stained clothes or clothes that need repair:** Donate or trash the stained clothing and put those "in-repair" clothes back in circulation. I hate mending clothing, but it's more efficient than having that item sit in a closet when it's otherwise perfectly appropriate to wear. Learn to sew on a button, stitch a tear in a seam, or have a seamstress, a tailor, your mom, your roommate, or someone do it for you.
- **Light wash, ripped jeans, or cut-offs:** If you work in an environment where your boss wears them, then it's acceptable. Typical offices draw the line at dark-wash denim, so look around before you wear them. Save the frayed short shorts for weekends.

- **T-shirts you bought at a concert, the beach, or a promotional event:** T-shirts that send a message (controversial or otherwise) with graphics or words are especially inappropriate for a professional environment. Unless there's a special event tying your organization to the promotion of that event—and t-shirts are part of it—keep them in your dresser drawer for after-work hours.
- **Anything that has sequins or sparkles:** Bedazzled doesn't befit a professional workplace. Save the bling for a corporate holiday party or the awards dinner that's scheduled *offsite*, in the *evening*.
- **Shorts, sandals, or flip-flops:** It's still important to follow dress codes and dress professionally in warmer months. Heat isn't an excuse to dress inappropriately. In some more casual business environments, women can wear shorts that reach the top of their knees, but men should steer clear of them entirely. Short skirts that show too much skin can be distracting and are fuel for gossip. As for flip-flops, it's hard for people to take you seriously when your presence is made known by the sound of flip-flops coming down the hallway. As for men, sandals give the same "too relaxed" impression when at work. Furthermore, socks with sandals is a clear fashion faux pas.
- **Anything you bought for the beach or pool:** Anything that says "beach" more than "boardroom" is not appropriate.
- **Unbuttoned shirts:** Guys who unbutton their shirts and show just a bit of chest hair have gone too far.
- **Sunglasses:** Don't wear sunglasses indoors, propped on your head all day. It looks ridiculous, and this isn't Hollywood.
- **Long dresses or cocktail dresses:** Floor-length dresses are appropriate only when the dress code says "resort wear." Dresses with satin, lace, beading, mesh, or fur trim are not appropriate for wearing to work in most industries.
- **Sneakers** (especially the Converse kind; my apologies to the Converse company but these sneakers are not appropriate for most business environments and that includes client outings at sports events...unless you're on the playing field or court!): As for other sneaker-type footwear, look around you to determine what is acceptable, check with human resources, or inquire about what has been set forth in the company dress code.

- **Cheap suits:** In a program recently, I felt a little guilty when one of the participants inquired about cheap suits, as he was newly hired and had a small budget for clothes. I always say, "Buy the best you can afford," but there's no reason to go broke buying clothes. Earlier in this chapter, I've included a section on **"How much should you spend?"** For now, remember that clothes are an *investment* when you begin your career. Look for quality in the construction, the fit, and choose high-quality fabrics that wear well and will hold their shape through numerous cleanings, like wool blends.

DRESSING FOR THE DUTY, NOT THE DAY

"If you've got a lunch meeting with a client...
don't forget to book style a place at the table."
—KENNETH COLE, AMERICAN DESIGNER

Clothes send a powerful message in business. People judge you by what you wear, and well-dressed people are promoted more often than those who dress too casual or sloppy. Politicians (especially female politicians) know that their style choices can potentially win or lose them votes. But just because you put on a sharp new suit for a job interview doesn't mean you don't have to prepare questions or do your homework on the organization.

One of the things students and emerging professionals want to know is *what* is appropriate for *when* in business. For example, it may be "dress down" Friday in our office, but if you're helping with the registration desk at a conference or attending an offsite meeting, does that mean you can automatically observe what's going on back at your office? Maybe not.

I've included a list of probable venues for most professionals and appropriate attire for each. What you wear sets the tone for business discussions, negotiations, and information exchange. The following pages will help you decide what *is* and what *is not* appropriate to wear in a professional environment, whether it's an internship, an interview, or at your job.

As a student-intern or new hire, you may be required to attend the following:

- ✓ Breakfast, lunch, or dinner meetings with clients
- ✓ Networking or industry events
- ✓ Outings with clients or client groups (sporting events, picnics, concerts, etc.)
- ✓ Sales presentations or company conferences
- ✓ Job interviews (internal or external)
- ✓ Holiday celebrations and special occasion office parties

BREAKFAST, LUNCH, OR DINNER MEETINGS WITH CLIENTS

Meetings with meals are really opportunities for your clients to affirm the notion that they made the right decision to hire your firm. At the table you'll be judged on your social savvy and your attention to detail. Your selection of attire is all part of that.

Observe the client's stated dress code if the meeting is a working meeting, but don't under dress.

OPTIONS FOR WOMEN:
- Nicely tailored slacks in a serious color such as gray, navy, or black
- Skirts no shorter than the knee
- Tailored jacket to coordinate (not necessarily match) your skirt or slacks
- Cardigan sweater set, pullover sweater (cashmere is a great investment), or basic white blouse
- Comfortable heels, simple jewelry, scarves, bold jewelry (lapel pins, necklaces, or bracelets that do not distract or jingle when you gesture)

OPTIONS FOR MEN:
- Suit or sport coat with dark khakis or dress trousers
- Long-sleeved button-down shirts
- Leather belts in black, brown, or burgundy to match your leather shoes with dark socks
- Fine-gauge sweater or sweater vest over cotton shirt; wrist watch in gold, platinum, or stainless with metal or leather band.

OPTIONS FOR BOTH: Topping your smart casual outfit with a blazer or sport coat even in a "roll up the sleeves" environment; a good quality pen, briefcase, or portfolio

---

NETWORKING EVENTS

Many students—both those serving an internship and those involved in campus organizations—are invited to go to networking or industry events so that they can get a "feel" for the business they are about to enter and build a connection with other professionals.

Most networking or industry events take place after hours. Professionals go from the office to the event and are usually in "business attire" or "business casual attire." There is always room for latitude depending on your industry. If you're serving an internship and are asked to attend a networking event, keep in mind that you will be going to the event straight from work and whatever you selected to wear in the morning will be worn for about twelve hours. Comfort is important, so this may not be the time to break in a new pair of shoes or wear something that's too restricting.

OPTIONS FOR WOMEN

- Basic day-to-night dress or pencil skirt with a blouse; dresses can be in a vibrant color with a fun detail at the neckline (bold or bright colors help you look approachable)
- Add a piece of statement-making jewelry like a gold cuff, ring, or necklace (sometimes a conversation starter)
- Well-fitted slacks paired with a blouse, sweater, or jacket with sleeves
- Heels if you've worn flats all day, or vice versa
- Portfolio or small purse—not both—with a side pocket (you'll be collecting business cards)

OPTIONS FOR MEN

- Suit or sport coat and dress trousers, with or without a tie
- Colorful pocket square or tie in good taste (remember, bold or bright colors help you look approachable)
- Button-down long-sleeved dress shirt or silk t-shirt under a blazer
- Business card holder (or a portfolio where you can collect business cards and keep yours handy to exchange; cards kept in a wallet tend to get folded, creased, torn, or dirty—not a good impression)
- Quality loafers or lace-up shoes worn with socks

OUTINGS WITH CLIENTS OR CLIENT GROUPS (SPORTING EVENTS, PICNICS, CONCERTS, ETC.)

One of my former students was hired to work for a large financial firm in Pittsburgh right after graduating from college. He knew he had a lot of opportunity for growth within the company. His company had season tickets for Pittsburgh Pirates games and he forced himself to go (even though he's admittedly an introvert), realizing this might be one of the only opportunities he would get to interact with corporate "higher-ups." In his position in the tech department, he rarely came face to face with the "C suite" executives, because he worked when the "big wigs" were out of their offices.

If you're not sure you want to attend a company outing, go anyway. Consider the benefit of interfacing with decision-makers in your company whom you wouldn't otherwise see and talk with. It's all part of networking, which we will address in Chapter 4.

In any event, just because it's a sporting event doesn't mean you have to be the mascot by painting your face in the colors of the team or [guys] removing clothes above your torso. When playoff time nears and especially on game day, tons of fans abandon otherwise social rules "just for the fun of it," and that's okay…when you're at home, with your friends, and your boss is miles away.

Many professionals do not realize these types of events can be a breeding ground for business mistakes. Combine a fun, casual setting with food and alcohol, and suddenly people let their guard down. Remember that it's still *business*. No matter the informality, you're there representing yourself to your company.

Continue to show team or corporate spirit. Participate in the games if it's appropriate but tone it down. It's not just about what you wear but also about how you act. Find a way to speak up if others encourage you to keep drinking after you've had enough (sneak away and secretly discard your drink) so that you don't have to apologize about your behavior on Monday morning.

OPTIONS FOR WOMEN

- Slim or cropped slacks with flats, wedges, or low-heeled sandals (nothing with a heel that can sink into the ground)
- Canvas sneakers or athletic shoes in good condition if you're going to be participating in some activities
- Bermuda or walking shorts (just above the knee)
- Sleeveless or short-sleeved cotton t-shirts or knit blouses with matching sweater if weather is chilly; no camisoles or strapless tops (A team jersey over a cotton t-shirt is also fine if you would normally wear a team jersey to a game.)
- Fitted cotton or denim jacket or blazer
- For any other items: select lightweight fabrics for summer, but not too sheer

OPTIONS FOR MEN

- A team jersey and cap is fine
- Polo shirt, cotton button-down, or nice t-shirt (not wrinkled and in good condition worn tucked or untucked)
- Khakis or your best denim jeans, belt preferred
- Khaki or cargo shorts, if the event is very casual (no "jorts"... jean + shorts)
- Docksides, low-top sneakers with shorts, loafers, sandals (out of these options, only sneakers really require socks that should be very short and come to your ankle or lower)

FOR BOTH

- Team jerseys are fine if you're a sports fan, but don't use this opportunity to sport a jersey for the rival team just to antagonize others, unless you know for certain the no one will be offended. Wearing a jersey for the opponent is fine, especially if it's your hometown. Wearing a jersey for any other team could be in poor taste, especially if the person who might be hiring you supports the rival team.

SALES PRESENTATIONS OR COMPANY CONFERENCES

Your image (how you look, move, etc.) will speak volumes about you before you open your mouth. Even if you're serving an internship as a student, it is important to look credible if you're asked to share your ideas or opinions, much less give a presentation at work.

Many professionals are so focused with pulling content together for a presentation, finishing slides, and practicing what they're going to say that they don't give a second thought to what they'll wear, until the last minute.

Plan. Select a tried and true favorite, or if you're buying something new, try on the whole outfit before the day of your big presentation so you can focus on what really matters: your message. Everything you say should be congruent with what you're wearing. You want to communicate capability, attention to detail, and credibility.

I've coached hundreds of students on presentations they give to corporate sponsors and mentorship organizations. In our coaching sessions, I always ask them what they will wear for their presentation. Particularly in a team presentation, I suggest that the students dress in a similar level formality. It's distracting to an audience and sometimes embarrassing to the student if one in the group is dressed in a suit and another is dressed in weekend wear. Yet, some students simply cannot afford to purchase a new outfit for an important presentation. Usually, we figure out a way to make it work, even if it means borrowing a sport coat, a pair of shoes, a necktie, or a blouse and jacket.

Try to wear something that distinguishes you from the audience when you're giving a presentation, whether it's in class or in a professional setting. In short, you want to try to be the best dressed person in the room when you're giving a presentation to a group—small or large.

OPTIONS FOR WOMEN

- Select clothes with natural fabrics that breathe: cotton, wool, silk.
- Select darker power colors (deep taupe, navy blue, charcoal grey) if you're presenting numbers and technical data to decision-makers.
- Select bright, vibrant colors if you're presenting a video conference or you'll be on TV; these colors look good to the eye and the camera. Don't wear white, black, or red. White glows and becomes the most noticeable thing on the TV screen. Black is too harsh and can suck up all the light. Reds bleed on camera and are distracting. Brightly patterned blouses with a solid suit or sweater are a good choice—especially for photos.
- Select more exciting and trendy colors if you're presenting to a company that is into the latest trends (show biz or retail clothing).
- Stay monochromatic (same color top and bottom) if you want to project a taller, slimmer silhouette.
- Keep jewelry simple; make sure nothing makes distracting noises.
- Pass on scarves or wraps unless they are well anchored; you'll no doubt be moving around as you present.
- Wear lipstick in a darker shade (so they can see your mouth) and foundation that matches your skin color. Eye makeup highlights the eyes and makes them more expressive.
- If you have long hair, make sure you're not constantly flipping and flinging it around (it's distracting for the audience to see that).
- Take a spare pair of pantyhose for more formal occasions, just in case.

OPTIONS FOR MEN

- A sport coat or blazer is a great equalizer; you can take it off if you feel overdressed or throw it on if you need to upgrade; button your jacket when you stand to speak. If your jacket has three buttons, the center one should be buttoned. If your jacket has two buttons, the top one should be buttoned.
- Wear a conservative long-sleeved button-down shirt that is well pressed, clean, and well fitted, preferably in white or light blue.
- Neckties: If you're presenting on TV or on a videoconference avoid fine patterns like herringbone or small checks as they can cause a wavy effect.
- Empty pockets before your presentation so you're not tempted to play with pocket contents.
- Hair should be neatly trimmed and in style.
- Have an extra tie or shirt handy just in case.

FOR BOTH

- Shoes should be well kempt, and heels should not be worn down. Shoes shouldn't squeak, flip-flop, or click when you walk around.
- If you're traveling any distance to a presentation, try to allow time to change into your presentation clothes when you arrive if you can find a private area. This will minimize wrinkles and avoid the possibility of picking up a stain during the journey. Nothing looks worse than presenters who look as if they've slept in their outfit.
- Dress in the color(s) of the client or organization. Selecting a color in their logo for your tie or blouse is subtle, yet strategic.

Formal Interoffice Job Interviews

As an intern, you may be asked to interview for a permanent position that gives you a salary and an official title. This is an occasion, and you should be dressed for it. It's better to risk overdressing than appearing too casual, even if the interview takes place in your internship location.

One of our valued clients, a director of human resources at a Fortune 100 company says, "Dress for an interoffice job interview as if you've never worked at the company before; as if it's the first time you walked in the door." I'll never forget her words.

OPTIONS FOR BOTH MEN AND WOMEN

- Suits are appropriate if you want to project formality and attention to detail. Select suits in less-severe colors such as brown, beige, light grey, medium blue, if the new job is informal. If you don't have a suit, borrow one from a same-sized friend and make sure it is clean and pressed.
- Plan to remove your jacket during the interview, so make sure your shirt or blouse has sleeves (long sleeves for men; short or long sleeves for women—no sleeveless) and is ironed.
- Wear formal dress shoes that are clean. Men, match your socks to your shoes and suit. Women, wear close-toed shoes and hosiery if you're wearing a skirted suit.
- Avoid new haircuts or styles. You don't want to distract too much from your regular look.
- Women, avoid brightly colored nail polish; tone it down for your interview. Men, avoid distracting-patterned ties and socks. You want the focus on your face.
- If you normally wear face jewelry, including nose and eyebrow piercings, and elaborate ear jewelry, select your least-distracting pieces for the interview.

The Exception to the Rule: Types of Jobs Where Business Casual Is Appropriate for the Interview

Keep in mind that in most business cultures, business casual *isn't* appropriate for a job interview even if it's acceptable once you get hired for a position. According to a survey at Clark University, a private research university in Worcester, Massachusetts, 81 percent of job recruiters indicated that professional business attire was the more appropriate dress for an office interview. In addition, 76 percent expected traditional business dress even if the office environment was casual dress.

Yet, not all jobs require the traditional "business suit" for an interview. Even if this is the case, it's still best to always stay away from trendy, sloppy, or too-casual clothes. Suppose you meet the president or CEO unexpectedly. You should look like you were ready to meet him or her even if you don't.

Job listings may recommend what is appropriate for the job interview, so check these out. If you determine that business casual is appropriate, wear clothes that are neat and clean, and make sure you are well groomed for the interview.

My father was a building contractor, and although he owned his own construction company, he worked side by side with his laborers on many occasions. He ate his lunch out of a brown bag and drank his coffee out of a thermos every day. He was a true example of the WWII generation, and a product of the Great Depression. "Honesty and hard work never hurt anyone," he'd say. His hands were calloused and rough from years of hard work up until the last years of his life when Parkinson's disease had him confined to a wheelchair.

My Dad was always hiring construction workers. One day, a young man with hair down to his shoulders knocked on the door of his office. When my Dad answered the door, the visitor said he was there to apply for a job. My Dad, without a moment's hesitation, replied, "We're not hiring secretaries" and immediately closed the door in the poor guy's face. Whenever I think about what to tell professionals to wear to a job interview where business casual dress may be appropriate, I think about that story (circa: 1980s) and my Dad's perception of shoulder-length hair on men.

Jeans, t-shirts, shorts, sneakers, and athletic wear are almost never appropriate unless you're specifically asked to dress that way. Remember that proper attire can help you make a good first impression. No one will ever fault you for "overdressing" to a job interview to appear professional.

Here are some interview situations where business casual *might* be appropriate:

- **Job fairs.** These are not formal interview situations and generally precede a formal interview, so business casual might be appropriate for a preliminary one-on-one interview. Some job fairs will suggest "interview attire" on their website so be sure to do your research in advance. Still, it never hurts to dress business professional at a job fair, especially if it will make you stand out. When my son Patrick was a freshman majoring in Business Technology Support, he was excited to attend his first job fair. He got a fresh haircut, then bought a crisp long-sleeved white and deep purple striped, fitted shirt with a solid purple tie. It was fun to text photos back and forth of the "finished" product. He looked great!

- **Worksite interviews.** Let's say you're working for a construction company and would like a position as a project manager. As an intern, you've been tasked to work "in the field" and wear workboots, goggles, and protective head gear. In this case, opt for business casual for your job interview if it will take place at, say, a construction site. Neckties, scarves, jewelry, and/or high heels could be a potential hazard.

- **Industry standards.** Pay attention to industry standards. For example, if heavy lifting, hands-on industry skills or outdoor labor is the norm, formal interview dress isn't expected. But don't relax too much. Remember the Clark University survey. Dress in smart casual or mainstream casual, at the very least.

BUSINESS CASUAL JOB INTERVIEW ATTIRE OPTIONS FOR MEN
- Pressed khaki or dark gabardine dress pants
- Blazers or sport coats in navy blue, black, or gray (dark colors create a more powerful presence than light colors)
- Collared shirts, button-down oxford or polo styles tucked into pants
- Polished leather loafers or dress shoes and matching belt
- Dark socks that are midcalf (we don't want to see that flash of skin when you cross your legs!)
- A conservative wristwatch is fine; remove earrings and try to cover tattoos
- Tie optional

BUSINESS CASUAL JOB INTERVIEW ATTIRE OPTIONS FOR WOMEN
- Khaki, twill, or cotton pants or skirts
- Casual knee-length skirts or dresses with sleeves
- Casual jacket or blazer
- Tailored knit sweaters or sweater sets; cardigans, polo/knit shirts
- Dark shoes; no strappy sandals or mile-high stilettos
- Stockings are not necessary for a business casual look
- Get or give yourself a manicure (simple, natural polish), and a pedicure if you are going to wear open-toed shoes
- Avoid pastel overload, see-through tops, uncovered cleavage, exposed undergarments, too tight pants, shimmering fabric, heavy makeup, flashy jewelry
- Solid colors work better than bright patterns

HOLIDAY CELEBRATIONS AND SPECIAL OCCASION OFFICE PARTIES

If you're interning at a company over the holiday season, chances are you'll be invited to the holiday soiree. Always dress like you have somewhere nicer to go to when you leave the party. As an intern, what you wear will be scrutinized more than most employees. The office holiday party is the perfect chance to show others you have class, so do it.

Give some consideration to what your spouse or significant other wears if he or she will attend your company's special occasion as your guest. The guests do not get an automatic pass to wear whatever they'd like just because it isn't *their* employer.

My friend's daughter was just hired by a sizable accounting firm, and she was told she could bring a guest to the new-hire reception and dinner offsite at an upscale venue. Her boyfriend <u>always</u> wears a baseball cap and claims it's a cover-up for premature baldness. My friend—a former educator—was concerned about the negative impression her daughter would make simply because her boyfriend was wearing a baseball cap (indoors) at a corporate event, which he did.

Sound farfetched? It's not. When attending any business event, the impression your companions make will reflect on you just as their behaviors reflect on you and your choices. *Your* dress code is *their* dress code. Their role is to support you and be gracious and engaging with the people you introduce them to. If they'd rather hog the food and get drunk, let them stay home.

The holiday office party is a place where things can really go awry. The combination of coworkers, cocktails, forced holiday spirit, and end-of-year stress is not always a good one. Think Christmas sweaters with blinking lights and fuzzy Santa hats. Think facing your boss or the HR department on Monday morning.

Office holiday parties can be more formal (cocktail attire) or less formal (casual family-friendly environment) so pay attention to the invitation to uncover any dress-code suggestions. When in doubt, ask someone who knows because they have attended year after year, or ask your boss. There's nothing wrong with asking someone; it shows your attention to detail, not ignorance.

Styles change as many times as the faces at your company. Many fashion retailers and magazines provide online articles with current trends and style suggestions for what to wear to your office holiday party. Always consider your professional style and how you'd like to be perceived (remember your three adjectives?), even in a party atmosphere. It's still business, so as an intern or new hire, you're going to be under a magnifying glass.

The more important message is *what NOT to wear to the office holiday party.* Refer to the beginning of this chapter and look again at my list of **what not to wear to work**. This list provides good guidelines for the office holiday party, except for sequins (for women). Also consider the **cost per wearing** formula to make sure you don't overspend.

WHAT NOT TO WEAR TO THE OFFICE HOLIDAY PARTY FOR WOMEN

- Outfits that reveal serious cleavage
- A pairing of holiday colors (e.g., a bright red skirt and a bright green sweater)
- The highest heels you own
- Micromini skirts or dresses
- Sheer fabrics or cutout dresses that expose a bare midsection or back
- Too much perfume
- Body glitter or skin sparkles
- Ultracasual attire
- Christmas sweaters that are in poor taste or battery operated (unless that is the theme of your party)
- Wrinkled or ill-fitting clothes
- Too tight skirts, blouses, or dresses
- Festive garb (antler headbands, Santa hats, mistletoe pins, battery-powered menorah necklaces); remember, people will be taking pictures
- Baggy, lighter wash denim (in most cases, dressing "down" instead of "up" at your holiday party will make you look lazy)
- Casual slip-on fur or fleece-lined boots (unless the environment is very casual)

WHAT NOT TO WEAR TO THE OFFICE HOLIDAY PARTY FOR MEN

- Mistletoe or tinsel anywhere on your body
- T-shirts or anything with a political message
- Anything that lights up: neckties, sweaters, sweatshirts, socks (Trust me, the battery will run out before the end of the evening anyway.)
- Jingle bells
- Holiday costumes (a cute Santa hat might be okay, but you don't have to wear the entire Santa costume, unless you've been asked to play Santa)
- Ultracasual attire
- Wrinkled clothing
- Cowboy boots
- Baggy, lighter wash denim

WHAT TO WEAR TO THE OFFICE HOLIDAY PARTY FOR WOMEN

- An updated "oldie but goodie." Update that same dress you've been wearing for years with a sparkly cardigan or tuxedo jacket, a holiday themed scarf, or colorful shoes.
- Hosiery: sheer black, lacy, opaque hose is acceptable.
- Proper undergarments: body shapers and control top pantyhose are a godsend under anything form fitting, especially evening wear.
- Pencil skirts with a silk blouse is acceptable.
- Dark washed jeans in a straight-leg style paired with a festive yet conservative blouse or sweater work best in a casual family-style environment.
- Dressy leather boots with heels also compliments most outfits.

DECIPHERING DRESS CODES

"I think clothes should make you feel safe."
—GILDA RADNOR

© Djomas/Shutterstock.com

A common grievance among young professionals and new hires is that dress code descriptors can be confusing. There are as many different dress codes as there are positions in an assembly line, and they each can have distinctive descriptions. I've detailed six different dress codes and compiled descriptors for each.

Corporate executives and human resource professionals don't love the task of writing dress code policies. It's not fun work. That's why many of our clients ask us to rewrite dress codes for them. Usually we find the existing policy is outdated or vague. Employees often misinterpret dress codes and managers are reluctant to speak to them about it because of the many ways the conversation could go wrong.

Before you review what is outlined here, remember that every company or organization has the right to set personal appearance and dress code standards for the employees who work there. Employers have the legal right to *reinforce* dress codes unless they discriminate against civil rights laws that protect an employee's gender or religious faith.

Ask for the dress code policy if you're a new hire or intern and ask questions if you're uncertain how to interpret it. You shouldn't have to guess. Then, dress *better* than the dress code's minimum standard and you can't go wrong. Most employers can provide a dress code to all employees regarding what's acceptable and unacceptable when it comes to wardrobe choices. Unfortunately, there is still that double standard between the sexes, as many image consultants suggest that *women should never dress as casually as men*.

When we write dress codes for our client companies, we consider two criteria:

Primary criteria:

1. The company's interpretation of business casual or business professional dress and when and where each is acceptable
2. The positions and responsibilities of their employees

Secondary criteria:

1. Their industry
2. Their geographic location with the United States or internationally

The attire clash between the West Coast and East Coast will become obvious if your job takes you between coasts. For example, a casual, unbuttoned look is great for the West Coast, while New Yorkers opt for more formal attire. West Coasters don't understand the importance Easterners place on dress. This could be to a fault, however, when in the case of a young executive who figured his single-breasted suit and tie would indicate that he was the more powerful guy in the room. To his clients in Beverly Hills, it indicated he was a "mid-level administrator"—somebody's accountant or agent. And that's fine, but he was aiming at something higher.

Neither coast has it all figured out, according to Parisian fashion experts who think all Americans dress like slobs. Even today, business casual is the exception, not the norm, in European and Asian cultures. The differences extend beyond New York and Los Angeles. The midwestern United States tends to be more conservative and preppy than either coast. In the South, there's more focus on color for both men and women.

More conservative industries include financial, legal, and some government organizations. More casual organizations tend to be non-profit, manufacturing, and educational groups. Among the least conservative are the arts, fashion, or music industries.

It's my observation regarding business casual dress in the United States that many employees (and employers who listen to them) are looking for an excuse to make their work environment like their "play" environment. Often, *casual* dress codes reflect that same mentality and put workers in the mindset to relax when they should not be. "Dressing down" does not mean dressing *down and out*. Don't be so quick to dress down; what you wear shows others that you respect them, and are prepared to tolerate mild discomfort (think hosiery, neckties, jackets) as a sign that you respect them enough to do so.

RESORT CASUAL

You'll see **"resort casual"** requested for offsite industry meetings, conferences, conventions, and corporate retreats and outings. Few people really know what it means. Resort casual is really "country club" wear. Even if you're not a member of a country club, you can probably guess that what you wear in a "private club" environment must be smart and refined. When dressing in resort casual for a business event, there are still some restrictions.

Resort Casual for Women

- Clean and pressed blouse paired with a nice pair of lightweight pants or skirt (watch hemlines; they should be at the knees or slightly above)
- Casual sheath dresses or knee-length sundresses in bold colors or prints that coordinate with your outfit and which are not too short or low cut

- Brightly colored good-quality t-shirts with crewneck or boatnecks and wide straps
- Cotton or linen blazers for daytime meetings if things are more formal
- Colorful wraps for evening functions
- Shorts that are longer in length and look good paired with a blazer
- Sandals (again, get or give yourself a pedicure)
- Well-fitted (not too tight) cropped pants which can be wide, tapered, skinny, flowy, or flared
- Tasteful straw hat with wide brim for beachside functions

Resort Casual for Men

- Clean and pressed button-down shirt or polo shirt
- Khakis or other quality pants worn with belts
- Good quality denim jeans in a dark shade that fit well may be appropriate for evening events but may not be appropriate in the daytime for business meetings or giving a presentation
- Light and bold-colored shirts in lightweight fabric such as linen are fine, if they are neatly pressed and well fitted (meaning, not too baggy or long)
- Quality silk-blend or cotton-blend t-shirts that can be paired with lightweight linen, cotton, or wool-blend blazers for evening functions (graphic t-shirts are not appropriate unless you've been told it's okay to wear a t-shirt with a relevant logo or design)
- Loafers and boat shoes are preferred over sandals for men at meetings (sandals or flip-flops may be appropriate for the beach or pool)
- Fedoras or brimmed straw hats (reintroduced as a fashion trend when Johnny Dep first sported the look in 2012) may be appropriate for the beach at a resort casual meeting but remember that is it never appropriate to wear a hat indoors. Current news on fedoras is that women don't really like them. If your boss is a woman, leave your fedora at home, in your closet.

SMALL BUSINESS CASUAL, AKA BASELINE BUSINESS CASUAL

You might be interning or working with a small business where the office is in the owner's home or a location away from where other businesses are located. That does not mean you can roll out of bed and go to work in your pajamas. The last time I was on an early morning conference call in my bathrobe, I didn't feel "on my game." But then again, I don't do business in a bathrobe unless I'm talking to clients on the opposite end of the world.

Small business casual does not mean sloppy or wrinkled clothing and overly revealing or offensive attire. Small business casual or baseline business casual is the norm in super-casual offices and is also appropriate if you're asked to work in your office on a weekend or help with cleaning or moving an office. Small business casual can also work when taking a client to a baseball game or attending the company picnic.

Small Business Casual for Women:

- Denim or cotton cropped pants or skirts
- Knit shirts or cotton blouses
- Casual closed-toe flats or slip-ons

Small Business Casual for Men:

- Well-tailored jeans (not the ones for yard work) or khaki pants
- Button-down shirts or knit polo shirts
- Casual slip-on shoes, preferably worn with socks

BUSINESS CASUAL OR SMART CASUAL

This is the term for standard business casual attire. When interning for a company that supports a casual dress code, remember that while that company wants their staff to be comfortable at work, they also want their staff to look professional.

Mainstream Business Casual for Women:

- Wool or good quality blended fabric skirt or slacks combined with coordinating blouses or tops
- Conservative dresses paired with a blazer or sweater
- Sweaters, cardigans, cropped cardigans
- Flat leather shoes, pumps, or boots
- Casual accessories (can include opaque hosiery)

Mainstream Business Casual for Men:

- Quality khakis, microfiber, or gabardine pants with solid or subtly patterned pressed cotton or cotton-blend button-down shirts
- Polo-style shirts, pullover sweaters
- Leather loafers or slip-on shoes

EXECUTIVE CASUAL

Executive casual is **business professional** with a more relaxed approach. This is a good look when you accompany your boss or a management-level group to a client meeting in a business casual environment. It's also appropriate to dress in **executive casual** when you give a presentation to senior managers who will be casually dressed.

Executive casual is the very dressiest of casual clothing. Here's where you need to pay attention to the quality of fabrics, your accessories, and how your clothes fit.

Executive Casual for Women:

- Higher-quality pant suits with silk, silk-blends, or cotton blouses
- Coordinated blazers
- Fine gauge cotton, cashmere, or cashmere blend wraps or full-length sweaters
- Quality low-heeled (two- to three-inch) pumps
- Understated accessories (real gold and silver is always appropriate)

Executive Casual for Men:

- High-quality fabric choices for cuffed, lightweight wool or wool-blend trousers with long-sleeved well-pressed shirts
- Fine-gauge cotton or cashmere/cashmere-blend sweaters
- Coordinated sport coats or blazers
- Leather loafers
- High-quality accessories (gold or silver watches with leather bands)

BUSINESS PROFESSIONAL OR TRADITIONAL BUSINESS

Guys, buy a neck tie. Business professional or traditional business means a suit and tie for men. Don't think that the popularity of business casual has dismissed the inclusion of the business professional or traditional business dress. It hasn't. For both men and women, there *will* be an occasion for you to wear a suit (consider job interviews, presentations, client meetings, global partner meetings), even if your organization has a casual dress code.

When it comes to business professional, be aware of appropriate colors that indicate a more powerful look. Choose medium to dark colors in shades of blue or gray. For women, lighter shades of camel or brown, as well as darker shades of burgundy, purple, green, navy, and gray are also appropriate for business professional.

Business Professional for Men:

- Wool or wool-blend suits in medium to dark colors (scrutinize how you look when trying on a suit and whether a "regular" or "slim" fit works best for your body type); also pay attention to sleeve length (shirt sleeves should protrude one-quarter to one-half inch from the jacket sleeves when you stand with arms hanging)
- White or blue business shirts with straight or spread collars (French cuffs are optional)
- Blazers paired with well-tailored trousers and button-down oxford shirts
- Silk tie (textured, plain, or with small, subtle pattern)
- Lace-up dress shoes
- Quality gold or stainless-steel watch or jewelry

Business Professional for Women:

- Suits or tailored separates
- Tailored business dresses with sleeves or paired with blazers or jackets
- Silk, knit, or cotton blouses or fine-gauged sweaters
- Quality low-heeled pumps

BOARDROOM ATTIRE OR BUSINESS FORMAL

As you begin your career, you're probably not going to be expected to wear **business formal** as it is the standard for CEOs and many "C suite"–level executives. Nonetheless, it's important for you to know the gold standard of professional dress that requires the highest quality fabrics, exceptional accessories, and the very best tailoring.

Business formal here does not dictate "black tie" as in the traditional sense. Remember, it's still tied to business. However, on the rare occasion when you receive a corporate invitation that reads "black tie," it means that men are expected to wear a tuxedo (rent one—don't think it's okay to go in your business suit) and women are expected to wear formal evening attire. Again, let good taste be your guide.

Business Formal for Women:

- High-quality skirted suits in wool or silk
- High-quality silk blouses
- Closed-toe pumps worn with pantyhose in a neutral shade
- Leather belts or silk scarves
- High-quality gold or silver accessories
- High-quality gold, silver, or stainless-steel watch

Business Formal for Men:

- High-quality dark wool suits and white cotton business shirts with straight collars (French cuffs are optional)
- High-quality silk tie
- Silk or linen pocket squares
- Lace-up shoes
- High-quality gold, silver, or stainless-steel watch

GROOMING AND ACCESSORIES

> *"Good grooming is integral and impeccable style is a must. If you don't look the part, no one will want to give you time or money."*
> —DAYMOND JOHN

© Africa Studio/Shutterstock.com

A college career counselor I interviewed for this book said her biggest pet peeve in how businesspeople look is sloppy grooming, "…from fingernails to hair down the back of men's necks." When people assess your competence and trustworthiness, grooming comes into play just as your clothes do.

What is the cost of poor grooming? Looking "polished" or "pulled together" is your most important physical asset, and it counts more than your weight or height. Interestingly, women are judged more harshly here. In a study found on Forbes online, 83 percent of senior executive said "unkempt attire" (including wrinkled or tight clothing and visible lingerie) detracts from a woman's executive presence; a slightly smaller percentage (76 percent) said it undermines a man's presence.

Most managers are tentative to address poor grooming because it's a delicate subject, it's embarrassing, and they're not sure how to say what should be said. They are happy to have the HR department handle any conversation regarding poor grooming or inappropriate dress, no matter how much coworkers are complaining.

We tend to notice grooming mistakes when we meet someone in a professional setting just like we remember bad customer service more often than good. It's easy to do because it's part of your first impression and it stands out.

Imagine how it feels to have a job interview with a potential employer and you're hoping he or she doesn't notice your chipped nail polish or that you need a haircut. Most of us barely have enough time to get all our work done, let alone pay attention to the small details of grooming like makeup, facial hair (men), breath, or our fingernails. Yet, attending to your grooming will be time well spent since it can show others that you also pay attention to detail in your work.

GROOMING MISTAKES

Poor grooming can turn off your coworkers, friends, and anyone you encounter in a one-on-one setting. Here is a list **grooming mistakes** that go with specific areas which support the rest of your appearance:

- **Hygiene:** Not wearing deodorant or antiperspirant daily or wearing a deodorant that does not stop wetness or odor; wearing clothes that haven't been laundered, cleaned, or aired out; wearing clothes that smell of smoke, mustiness, or unpleasant food odors (spicy foods may increase the odor associated with perspiration); for women, not removing underarm hair (it's a breeding ground for bacteria according to medical experts).
- **Teeth:** Not brushing or flossing properly to remove tartar; not using teeth whitening products; having very crooked, discolored, or missing teeth; not getting your teeth professionally checked and cleaned at regular dental appointments (usually twice a year).
- **Breath:** Not using mouthwash; not using a tongue scraper (most bad breath starts here); eating foods that cause bad breath (e.g., caffeine, sugary foods and drinks, garlic, onions, acidic foods like tomatoes, peppers, vinegar, and citrus fruit)

- **Facial hair (men):** Visible nasal or ear hair; sporting a "unibrow" or bushy eyebrows; not shaving your neck when you have a beard; not trimming your beard; facial hair that does not compliment your face type; shaving with a dull blade or not replacing rotary and foil blades on your electric shaver to get a clean shave; having food stuck in your mustache/goatee/beard.
- **Hairstyle (women):** Unkempt hair; untrimmed bangs; dirty hair; lazy or dated hairstyles (ponytails, hair twisted into hair clips); unplucked or undefined and trimmed eyebrows; grown-out highlights or hair color (have your hair colored or trimmed every six to ten weeks).
- **Hair (men):** Too much hair product; haircuts that do not compliment your face or are not age appropriate; sporting a combover; not maintaining your style between cuts; not shampooing daily to eliminate oiliness, dandruff and flakes; not using a hair conditioner; long bushy sideburns; unnatural hair coloring.
- **Fingernails:** Fingernails that have been bitten; dry or cracked cuticles; bleeding cuticles; dirty fingernails (from grease, gardening, home projects, etc.); chipped nail polish; nails that are long enough to be lethal weapons; nails/hands in need of a manicure (both men and women—manicures are not just for women), nails that are different lengths, chapped, dry, or cracked hands.
- **Skin:** Acne; blackheads; oily skin; inflamed skin; not exfoliating lips; not cleaning your ears properly, using a cheap self-tanner or too much self-tanner (you look orange); razor burn or whisker stubble (men).
- **Clothing:** Clothes that don't fit properly or need to be altered (suits, slacks, blazers or sportscoats, pants, dresses); not having a sharp crease in pants or slacks; wrinkled, stained, soiled, or torn clothes; missing buttons; falling hems; not handling or storing clothes properly (e.g., hanger indentations on blouses or sweaters from wire hangers); frayed hems or cuffs on slacks; not wearing belts with slacks or pants that have belt loops.
- **Underwear:** <u>For men,</u> not wearing a V-necked undershirt beneath an open-collared dress shirt or wearing a t-shirt with graphic images that show through a dress shirt. <u>For women,</u> visible bra or camisole straps that are really underwear; visible panty lines; underwear (in particular, a thong) that shows above the top of slacks or pants when bending over.
- **Hosiery and socks:** Runs, snags, bags, wearing low-quality socks (causes smelly feet); short socks that display a hairy leg

when seated (men), wearing white socks (men), not wearing hose with a skirt for an important business meeting (women).

- **Shoes:** Badly worn heels; unpolished shoes; scuff marks; cloth or canvas shoes with holes; all-white shoes (unless you are wearing all white); shoes that are a lighter shade than your slacks, skirt, or dress; wearing sneakers or sporty shoes with a suit.
- **Makeup:** For women, not wearing any makeup (see makeup basics for women sidebar). For men, not wearing a loose translucent powder to control and absorb oil if you have very oily skin. For both, not using a spot concealment for blemishes and/or visible spot concealer that is not blended into natural skin tone.
- **Fragrance:** Wearing too much cologne or perfume (many work environments are fragrance free); wearing a cologne or perfume just because of the brand name; wearing a fragrance on a job interview (you never know if your interviewee is allergic to fragrance—don't chance it).
- **Jewelry:** Too much jewelry (rings on each finger, multiple piercings); jewelry that is oversized and noisy; jewelry that interferes with the use of hands; poor quality or cheap jewelry; wearing sport watches with business professional attire; earring(s) for men in conservative professional environments (do some homework and find out what is acceptable in the business environment you'll be working in).

MAKE UP BASICS FOR WOMEN:
- a foundation that is close to your natural skin color
- a burgundy-toned blush
- a powdered eye shadow to highlight and emphasize your eyes
- a black or brown-black mascara
- lipstick in a color that will flatter your teeth and work with your coloring

- **Eyeglasses:** Tinted eyeglasses or sunglasses indoors; dirty eyeglasses; eyeglasses with glare (always select nonglare), distracting eyeglasses with too much bling (for women); eyeglasses with too large frames (no matter the trend, small frame glasses are a more professional look for both men and women); eyeglasses that are not fitted properly or are not flattering to the shape of your face.
- **Tattoos, body piercings, visible body art:** Revealing a tattoo at casual corporate events when you usually keep it covered; revealing additional piercings at casual corporate events when you haven't shown them before. Understand your company's policy on tattoos or body piercings if there is one. While some dress codes

outlaw visible tattoos at work, others allow them—if they are tasteful and not offensive to others. If you don't know, ask someone you respect. And until you're certain, do not use the corporate picnic or casual event as your "outing" when showing tattoos and multiple piercings for the first time.

Many students would like me to tell them tattoos, blue or purple hair, and multiple piercings are becoming more acceptable in the workplace nowadays. According to the Equal Employment Opportunity Commission (EEOC), companies can limit employees' personal expression on the job if those expressions do not impinge on their civil liberties. The visible tattoo may be losing its taboo status, but if a company feels strongly that having tattoos and excessive piercings might hurt their company's image and influence their customers' level of comfort when dealing with employees, they then have a strong legal basis for asking an employee to keep tattoos covered. As an intern or new hire, you are not protected by the First Amendment in this case.

ACCESSORY ETIQUETTE

I have a valued client who is a manger for a non-profit organization. Her nails are a work of art—each one—and her hoop earrings could easily be a chain belt for one of my skinniest friends. This is her style, and one that she says identifies her culture. However, when she gives a presentation to her directors or attends a fundraiser for her non-profit, she replaces her hoop earrings with more subtle ones, and has her nails polished in a neutral shade. She tones it way down to be on the safe side.

Accessories provide an opportunity for you to put your personality into what you wear. They can also indicate your individuality. Quality, understated accessories don't go out of style, so you can justify spending a little more on them. If you don't have a budget for real silver or gold, look for pieces that are on sale to compliment your outfits.

© berezandr/Shutterstock.com

BEST IN CLASS

In general, accessories should be understated in the workplace. If you wear too much or too many, people may perceive you as "flashy." If you wear too few, people perceive you as having no style and perhaps being too conservative.

A good rule of thumb for women to follow is the <u>Rule of Thirteen.</u> Count the number of accessories you're wearing from head to toe. Include scarves, headbands or hair ornaments, earrings, rings, ornate buttons, belts, even shoes with silver or gold pieces, and eye glasses. If the number is higher than thirteen, you're probably over doing it.

ACCESSORY OPTIONS FOR WOMEN

Purses, briefcases, and backpacks. In business, the more "stuff" you tote around with you the less in control you appear to others. That's why you'll need a bag that is suitable to take to work and that holds all your work essentials. Select a briefcase, portfolio, backpack, or a simple understated leather tote with pockets for all the unnecessary items you'll probably never ever use but like to have!

It may be hard to pare down to one handbag/briefcase/portfolio/bag that will keep you organized and looking good. The backpack you carried in college covered with nylon, reflective material, and bungee cords doesn't exactly pair well with the more professional attire you'll be wearing to work. Consider a more mature-looking work bag made of premium leather or waxed canvas in a neutral color and a smart, low-key design that is stylish and functional. Designer handbags may look good, but there's only so much they can hold, and the thin straps on many such bags may not wear well.

Choose sleek, understated yet functional and simple cases for mobile devices and notebooks or if you carry a laptop to work, choose a work bag with a dedicated laptop compartment so your device is protected. Keep your bag clean, organized, and in good condition.

Jewelry. Invest in quality jewelry, and you'll want to wear it often. It always looks good and it doesn't wear out. Costume jewelry can also look good and there are many quality brands. I'm prone to losing "real" pieces, so I don't take good jewelry with me when traveling. Fashion forward jewelry may not compliment conservative business attire that you'll wear for a job interview, so stick to the basics and remember the "Rule of Thirteen."

It may help you to determine whether you look better in gold or silver. You can test yourself by holding a gold earring at one ear and a silver earring at another. Which one looks better with your skin tone? If you can't decide, take off your makeup, tie your hair back, and repeat this test. Once you've made your decision, factor this into other purchases like belts, buttons, and hardware on purses, even trim on shoes.

Earrings are a good thing, and they'll always fit no matter your size! An image consultant I know always recommends earrings because they add visual balance to a woman's total look. She also says that simplicity in neckwear—or the choice not to wear it—can enhance a quality outfit and bring focus to your face. I'm five feet four inches tall and sometimes would like to project a taller silhouette, so I chose pendant necklaces rather than something closer to my neckline.

Scarves, belts, hats. I love scarves, and they're still in fashion. The trending may change from skinny scarves to some that are a bit more dense, but this small accessory can change your look dramatically. Oblong scarves are the most versatile, and scarves come in a variety of materials from silken to cotton and knit blends. You can even wear scarves as a belt.

I rarely get rid of scarves because they can update an outfit or pull one together, adding an accent color to sharpen your look. Stars like Christina Aguilera add punch to their already fabulous purses by fastening designer scarves to their bags. For business, scarves can replace neckline jewelry, tied either in the front, side, or back.

Belts are a great fashion-find and can complement and update an outfit, if you buy the right kind for your body type. Wide stretch belts work well on anyone with a full waist and they can also highlight hourglass and pear body shapes. They are not good for short-waisted shapes. Skinny belts are ideal for adding a sophisticated, smart, and elegant feel to a suit or a pair of slacks and they are the optimum choice for a short-waisted or petite body figure.

Hats are not an appropriate accessory for women in business unless you're at a casual business-social outing or at a resort. Besides, who wants "hat hair"? Hats in cold weather make sense, however, so select one that looks good on you and does the least amount of damage to your hair.

Head wraps. Black women have long celebrated their culture and pride with intricate wraps of fabric. Head wraps have a long and complicated history and mean far more than a piece of fabric wound around the head. Before you consider that a head wrap is appropriate in the office, remember that you may still have to contend with stares, uninvited comments, and criticisms of coworkers, higher-ups, and people who just don't know any better.

ACCESSORY OPTIONS FOR MEN

A couple of years ago I found a survey that mentioned how the watch a man wears and the pen he uses are the accessories that most often get noticed. For example, some image consultants will advise men to wear no more than three accessories for a job interview (i.e. watch, belt, ring).

Backpacks and briefcases. Guys have stuff, too, and chances are that you've been carrying a backpack all through college. Some professionals say that a backpack makes you look "like a college kid touring Europe trying to find a youth hostel," but others do not think it matters. Attaché cases or briefs with handles seem to say, "I'm ready for business."

A traditional backpack might not be appropriate if you'll be wearing a suit or a blazer. First, the shoulder straps of the backpack will ruin the shoulder pads in your blazer and wrinkle your jacket. If you're wearing a suit, carry a bag by the handles, which means you'll need a briefcase. A smaller folio that carries your laptop and a few essentials can give a more professional image, especially on a job interview. There are many professional-looking backpack options.

Whatever you choose—backpack, messenger bag, folio—invest in something that meets your needs. Consider what you're going to put in your bag (technology, lunch, water bottle, gym clothes for after work, papers, etc.). Keep your pack simple and efficient; no bright colors, prints, or patterns. Limit yourself to one or two exterior pockets (no water bottle holders). Choose one that is in a shade compatible to your everyday business attire (i.e., black, brown, grey, or burgundy). Worn briefcases can have an austere sophisticated look, but make sure yours is in good condition; holes and tears repaired, tattered corners mended (not with duct tape), etc. Like all of your accessories, the condition of them will show your attention to detail.

Ties, belts, shoes. Ties decorated with cartoon characters, golf tees, or wildlife paintings are not going to go well with any suit or sport coat, so don't buy them. Select quality "updated" ties that can be tied in a strong knot. Smaller patterned ties project more authority. If you're giving a presentation as part of your job interview, select a tie in a brighter color. Pocket squares (or what was previously known as a handkerchief) are a symbol of a well-dressed man, according to style consultants. Pocket squares can be in almost any fabric as long as they're thin enough to fit in the breast pocket of your blazer or suit jacket when folded and not bulge out.

Belts and shoes should match in color, if not material. Lace-up shoes are more conservative than loafers. The biggest mistake most guys make is to wear loafers with a business or evening suit.

There is more to belts for men than fit and quality. Belts and pants should match formality; narrow belts with dressy pants and wider belts with casual pants (chinos, khakis, jeans). If you're tall or have a large frame, go with a larger buckle. If you're not, go with one that's smaller and more decorative.

Watches and wallets. With all the technology today, some men (and women) combine fitness trackers with smartwatches, if they wear one at all. A watch is a great business accessory, no matter how many gadgets you carry with you that tell time. Try to wear a good-quality watch with a leather or metal band. Fitness trackers or smartwatches that have colorful plastic silicone wristbands, obvious blinking or bleeping lights, and blatant LED light-up screens may be more distracting than impressive as an accessory. Regarding jewelry, use the one-ring maximum, on one finger. High school and college rings may not be appropriate for a sophisticated business look.

Think about these two situations: First, a man takes out his wallet; it's frayed, held together with a rubber band, and bursting with receipts. Second, the same man takes out a wallet, but it's sleek, in a dark leather, slim, and looks both stylish and expensive. Wallets should be functional and have some degree of style to convey how you want to be perceived, and they don't need to be very expensive. There are many styles of wallets, from the classic American billfold to the more cosmopolitan travel wallet, and the simple money clip. Whatever wallet you choose, choose something you really like. A wallet, like your most personal accessories, should be an investment.

GETTING THE BEST FIT OFF THE RACK FOR WOMEN

When it comes to fit, never go by the size of the garment. Different manufacturers have different size scales that can vary the fit...sometimes as much as two sizes! Still, if the garment does not fit, try another on in the same size even if they are labeled the same.

Always try garments on before buying them, especially skirts and pants. Look at the back view first, because it's very telling. Skirts should not hike up in the back at your waist level. Is the item pulling anywhere? Check the hem of your skirt or dress to see if it is straight. The front of your blouse or blazer should not gape at the bust level. Ask yourself how the item feels. Sit down and bend over in the garment. Cross your legs as you're seated. Garments should be gently molded to your body, but not constraining or take on a shape of their own when you move about.

FINDING THE RIGHT FIT FOR MEN:
SUITS, SHIRTS, AND PANTS

Properly-fitted suits can make a big difference in your overall appearance and your stature. My son, a network administrator, wore a suit for his job interview even though he knew his employer would likely never see him in a suit again until someone's funeral. Problem was, he had lost about twenty-five pounds in six months following the suit purchase and, according to him, said his pants looked like MC Hammer in a music video. Fortunately, his jacket still fit well across the shoulders, and he wore his pants with a belt and kept his suit jacket buttoned.

If you're buying a suit there's one place you should always start when determining a proper fit: the back of the coat. If it doesn't fit from shoulder to shoulder, the best tailor in the world can't fix it. For sleeves, there should be four inches from the bottom of the thumb to the bottom of the sleeve. Today, everyone wants to look taller and slimmer, so your suit jacket should be an inch longer than the bottom of the fingers when the arms are down, in a relaxed position.

For pants, wear the shoes you'll use with the pants. The waistband on your slacks should hit you at the waist, not the hips. The bottom of the trouser should cover the top half of the shoe and a slight break in the trouser over the shoe is preferable.

Pleats, flat-front pants, cuffed, or uncuffed pants are all matter of personal choice. Consider your build and height. Generally cuffed pants convey a less formal look. (Tuxedo trousers are never cuffed, for example.)

When buying a dress shirt, slip two fingers between your neck and the buttoned collar, and the shirt will fit comfortably after laundering. Shirt cuffs should extend one-half inch beyond your suit jacket sleeve. White and light blue shirts still are the most professional and conservative colors for wearing with suits. Whether you choose a spread collar, button-down, or pointed collar is a matter of choice and also what works best with the style of your suit or sport coat. French cuffs are for the most professional look and should never be worn with a sport coat just the same as short-sleeved shirts should never be worn with a suit.

Recently I helped a young engineer with his wardrobe and our biggest learning curve was that he saw how much more trim he looked in flat-front pants over pleated-front pants. He would never have considered flat-front pants; he was so accustomed to the comfort of pleated pants. However, buying the right fit pant put all of that to rest. He's now a convert to flat-front pants.

Some manufacturers sell suits that can be interchanged; you can wear a jacket as a sport coat or with trousers from another suit. This helps if you're on a tight budget and will need to wear a suit or sport coat frequently in your internship or job. Just make sure that it *is* versatile. Usually, a suit is a suit and a sport coat is a sport coat.

That's a Wrap

People make ten judgments about you in the first few minutes they meet you, and how you're dressed is one of them. Your dress and your grooming say a lot about your mood, energy level, and attitude.

Fashion crimes are easy to commit. Freedom of dress is not a right guaranteed by the Constitution. In most every organization, a dress code will still carry limitations, even in business casual environments. The subtle messages you send with the way you dress can and will impact your success in the workplace. Don't chance it by wearing something you *think* should be appropriate.

Give what you're going to wear a second thought, or it could be your peril. As you start your career, remember that it's not *your* company (yet) and you don't have the right to start a new dress code just because you landed the job. Dress to <u>support</u> your information and intelligence. It will take potential employers and other professionals a lot less time to make a positive decision about you if *you* take the time to give special consideration to your appearance.

COMMUNICATION SIGNALS

© pathdoc/Shutterstock.com

In my business communication class, we do an in-depth study of communication signals as we begin our public speaking unit. I ask my students to brainstorm all **visual, vocal, and verbal signals** that have the potential to alter or influence communication, and then break them down.

Visual Signals and Body Language

Being a man of small stature, Napoleon's height was not an advantage when he communicated with his armies. But his eye contact was.

Fact is, height *does* give you an edge when you're trying to project a powerful image along with many other visual signals. Taller candidates have won 58 percent of the U.S. presidential elections between 1789 and 2008. Taller people convey a sense of leadership, according to some researchers who say that leftover caveman instincts draw us toward strong and mighty (or tall) leaders who we view as able to protect us. But height isn't the only thing.

Dress and accessories. Try to look polished. It signals to others that you see them as worthy of your time and investment. Don't confuse the "bar" with the "boardroom," and don't continuously touch your accessories, hair, or anything (especially above your neck); it's perceived as fidgeting.

Stance and posture. Stand tall. The old "book on the head" technique you may have heard from your grandmother has merit because it straightens your back and aligns your head with your shoulders. You will look better, feel better, breathe better, and show more energy.

To know how this feels, stand with your back against the wall, making sure that both shoulder blades are touching the wall and the back of your head is also touching the wall. Keeping this same posture, take a step forward. Then, walk this way when you enter a room for a job interview or an important meeting. Interviewers make hiring judgments within the first ten seconds of meeting you and how you walk into the room is part of that judgment. No matter how you feel inside, standing straight and tall communicates confidence.

Gestures. Show and use your hands. Any image consultant will tell you that when your hands are visible, you look more powerful. When you speak naturally, you use your hands freely. Even blind people gesture.

Many of my students think they use their hands too much, especially when they stand in front of the class to give a presentation. I *rarely* see excessive gesturing, even from students who say, "I can't help it—I'm Italian!" Using your hands when speaking also helps you find the right words and expand your vocabulary, as proven in a study by the American Psychological Association. Plus, it helps you relax even when you're seated like in a job interview situation.

Facial expressions. Smile more and you'll sound better. Facial expressions have a direct link to the way your voice sounds. Picture the professor with a monotone voice (my students tell me there are many). What is this person's facial expression? It's probably blank.

The human face makes twenty-one different emotional expressions, each one different from the other. Controlling the face can help control the mind, according to an article published by *Time* in 2009. In that article, psychologists referenced a *Science* paper published in 1983, which revealed that "those instructed to produce certain facial movements showed the same physiological responses as those asked to recall a highly emotional experience."

One of the most powerful ways to establish instant rapport with someone you meet is to smile, and the smile has its place in business as well. Of course, you wouldn't use the smile to communicate bad news to a colleague, but you *would* use it when you're meeting someone for the first time, beginning a presentation, or at a business event when you want to look approachable. Have someone record you when you're giving a presentation or observe when you use Facetime or Skype to see if your facial expressions enhance or detract from what you're saying.

Eye communication. Look people in the eye when you meet them. Like Napoleon claimed, eye contact communicates understanding. It also communicates acceptance and that is why looking people in the eye when you first meet them is critical.

Eye contact is also one of the most important persuaders in business. In the American business culture, *staring at someone* means that you either want to "date" them or "fight" them. (To avoid staring, look at different parts of the person's face every two seconds, rotating from eyes, to nose, to lips, to chin, to cheeks, to forehead, etc.)

When we lack confidence or are uncertain, we naturally avert eye contact We blink, or look up or down. We also break eye contact when we feel a connection kick in. Make direct eye contact with the person(s) you're speaking to for only a moment longer, then break away to show just the right level of engagement. Your eyes are the window to your interest level, confidence, and professionalism during a job interview. When you establish good eye contact, you'll feel heard and appear likeable.

Distractions. Every person has physical habits. Some people fidget. Some people slouch. In other people, there may be disturbing gestures. These habits can emerge in critical situations, like a job interview when you have nervous energy and a natural desire to do your best. Unfortunately, they can be distracting and cost you the job.

Here are some visual signals to avoid during a job interview:

- *Playing with your hair, fingernails, or jewelry.* Avoid rings, watches, and jewelry if you're prone to playing with them. Tie your hair behind your back. If it's not there, you won't play with it.
- *Invading personal space.* Be aware of your interviewer's personal space. Ask where you should sit; don't just plop down on the first available chair. Don't stand too close and don't place your objects on top of the interviewer's things or move his or her things to make space for yours.
- *Crossing your arms.* This makes you look defensive or uncomfortable. We tend to pull ourselves together when we don't feel secure. Use your hands to gesture and you'll appear more enthusiastic and engaging.
- *Hiding your hands.* Place your hands on the top of the conference table or on the arms of your chair instead of hiding them in your lap.
- *Fidgeting.* This is a distraction and a sign of anxiety. Don't touch your face, play with objects or accessories, jiggle change in your pocket, or constantly click your pen.
- *Bad posture.* Sit with your back straight against the chair or stand up straight. Body posture has a lot to do with your listening skills, and asymmetrical body language can make you look dishonest, confused, or bored.
- *Lack of eye contact.* As mentioned, think of eye contact as a connection tool.

- *Weak handshake.* Make sure your handshake is firm, but don't give the hiring manager a "bone crusher." Keep in mind that appropriate pressure varies from culture to culture.
- *Excessive head nodding.* Nod your head occasionally to show you agree or understand what is being said, but don't nod excessively.

Cameras don't lie. Get a good friend to practice with you answering interview questions and recording your answers on your phone. Play it back and forth and watch for habits that might be distracting. It's hard to see yourself on video as others see you, but until you do, you'll never know what visual signals might be taking away from the positive image you want to project. Remember that negative differentiators, like poor and ineffective body language, help make the decision easy for the hiring manager.

VOCAL SIGNALS AND HOW YOU SOUND

"Words mean more than what is set down on paper. It takes the human voice to infuse them with deeper meaning."

—MAYA ANGELOU

© Syda Productions/Shutterstock.com

The sound of your voice, more than any other communication signal, translates emotion. Watch a television show in another language and I'll bet even though you can't understand what they're saying, you can get the gist of what's going on by just listening to the voices.

You've heard the expression, "It's not what you say but how you say it." That refers to how you sound, and can include your voice tone, pitch, rate, and volume as well as how you emphasize words and when you take pauses.

When you communicate in business, pay attention to how you sound. Record your voicemail on your phone in your *own* voice, don't use the "default" voicemail recording. You'll get an idea of how you sound to others. Your phone may be your best vocal coach, so use it to record yourself speaking sounding more powerful and confident, not rushed. If you're waiting for a call back from a potential employer, remember that your voice mail can be their first impression of you.

As a music major in undergraduate school ions ago, I minored in voice. My voice teacher said if you want to change the sound of your voice, change how you breathe. When you get nervous, your voice gets squeaky and high, not the confident image you want to project in a job interview. The cure is breathing low, using your abs to push down and relax. Also let your throat be open and free of tension. (An open throat produces a richer sound.)

THE FIVE "Ps" OF VOCAL VARIETY: PITCH, PUNCH, PAUSE, PACE, PASSION

When face to face or on the phone, vocal variety is key to a powerful voice. Here are five "Ps" of vocal variety:

Pitch. Speak too low and nobody will hear you. Speak too high and you may sound nervous. Your natural pitch is where you'll sound best. To find your natural "pitch," start humming "Happy Birthday." Stop on the first note and start speaking in that same pitch.

Punch. Punch is the accent or emphasis you place on a word or words. When you do this, your voice communicates specific meanings. The best example I can think of for "punch" is a TV meteorologist (weatherperson). Listen to them deliver the weather, and you'll hear them use a lot of punch and pitch variety to hold the interest of the viewer.

Pause. You should build pauses into your speaking, but not too much unless you're giving a presentation. A few well-timed pauses will give you a chance to think about what you've said or what you're going to say and in turn, give the other person(s) a chance to do the same.

Pace. Speaking too fast can make you sound nervous and wear out your listeners. On the other hand, speaking too slowly might make you sound less intelligent or tentative.

Passion. Passion is an all-important quality when you want to make a good impression. Love what you say about yourself in a job interview and love what you say about your topic when you're giving a presentation.

In your vocal communication, you'll want to avoid the tragic trio of these three "power robbers":

Up-speaking. This is the rising intonation at the end of a declarative sentence. Up speaking is when you *sound* like you're asking a question but rather, you're making statement. It turns every sentence into a question. Linguists have studied "upspeak," finding that it occurs most frequently among younger individuals and among women.

A lot of young professionals don't realize they up speak. It's annoying to listen to and not easy to change. When you upspeak, you run the risk of sounding unsure of what you're saying, and it's a liability when you're sharing your opinions or suggestions. Aim to pitch your voice downward at the end of a sentence to sound more authoritative.

Native accents. The world would be boring if we all sounded the same, but native tongues get in the way of communication. That's why you don't hear native accents on television among news anchors or re-porters. If you can't *tame* your native tongue, spend a few sessions with a voice coach who can give you the basic sounds of English and help you pronounce specific words by modeling them for you.

Trailing off. One of the first things I notice when I begin a semester with a new class of students is that many do not speak loudly enough in class. Many of them also "trail off" and decrease their volume at the end of the sentence as if they just "died on us." My theory is that they're not sure if they're finished speaking, so they just fade out. Here again, it appears as if you're unsure of yourself and what you're saying when you trail off. So, stay strong.

Avoiding the **tragic trio** and changing any one of the Five "Ps" will give you vocal variety and power in how you sound. The most important thing is to be authentic. Seek feedback, listen to yourself, and make changes according to how you'd like to sound.

VERBAL SIGNALS AND POWER WORDS

"...choosing the right words is harder than I thought."
—Cynthia Lord

© bleakstar/Shutterstock.com

Verbal signals include your choice of words and how you structure them into sentences.

Years ago, there was a Miss America pageant contestant who babbled and rambled her way through the "on stage" question. She talked incessantly but said nothing that made sense. The video went viral and was no doubt an embarrassment for her and the Miss America organization. Later, on some talk shows, she got an opportunity to revive herself and proved that nervousness, not a lack of intelligence, prompted her botched response.

The words you use when you speak say a lot about you. Use poor grammar and people will think you're uneducated. Use slang and they think you grew up in the "backwoods" or are just plain lazy.

When I ask my students how many use a thesaurus or a word-finding app when writing a paper, almost all hands go up. When I ask how many use a thesaurus or a word-finding app to find the right words when they're giving a presentation, almost no hands go up. At the end of this chapter, you'll see a list of "Power Words According to Industry." It's worth seeking out the right words to be more powerful when you give a presentation, speak up at a meeting, or speak up in class. At other important times, whether you're speaking to a hiring manager, your professor, or an industry professional, words can *make you* or *break you*.

Here are some **verbal signals** to consider:

Descriptive, simple language. Many of my students hate it when professors use words they *know* the students will not understand. Students hate it more when the professor does not provide a definition. Use simple, descriptive language in your speech so that people understand you.

Short sentences. Shorter sentences, when speaking, are more easily understood. Consider the speaker who rambles on and can't finish a sentence. We lose interest in midsentence. Jerry Seinfeld, the comedian, was known to mark up the scripts his writers would give him before he did a comedy routine. The writers would become annoyed; they put a lot of time into selecting precise wording to get the intended reaction. They would ask him why he was redoing their work and crossing out words to make sentences shorter. He said, "It gets me to the punch line quicker." He was right. Get to the punch line quicker.

Avoiding tag questions. A tag question is a statement followed by a mini question. We use tag questions for confirmation or to encourage a reply from the person(s) we are speaking to. A few tag questions to encourage a reply are fine. An example might be, "It's beautiful weather outside, *isn't it?*" or "That test was really hard, *wasn't it?*" When you use a tag question after every sentence, it can become annoying and distracting.

Avoiding qualifiers. Qualifiers are words that create doubt or uncertainty. Consider when you're shopping at a store (does anybody do that anymore?) and the clerk approaches you and says, "May I help you?" The classic response is "No thanks, I'm *just* looking." That little word *just* is a qualifier, the same as it is an apology on the telephone when you call to say, "I'm *just* calling to find out about available internships." Qualifiers can be weak, and they leave people wondering if you really know what you're talking about. Other qualifiers to avoid using frequently are:

basically	*essentially*	*sort of*
probably	*generally*	*virtually*
possibly	*kind of*	*a lot*
may	*mostly*	*really*
might	*rather*	*very*
could	*slightly*	
maybe	*hopefully*	

If you're using qualifiers because of a lack of confidence, ask yourself: What do I need to do to feel more confident with my information? Do I need to get feedback from someone I trust to feel comfortable with how I speak?

Avoiding trigger words. A trigger word can initiate a process or course of action. Trigger words can be both positive (to move someone to action or reaction) and negative. Negative trigger words cause negative emotions or reactions to them. Consider a restaurant review for a new bakery. In the review, the words *tasteless, dry, overpriced* were used to describe the cupcakes. There are also trigger words you should avoid in an email so that you don't sound insincere. Here are some:

> **Any words ending in "n't"**—They connote negative meanings and should be avoided in an email you'd otherwise like to keep positive (e.g., *don't, won't, can't, couldn't, wouldn't, shouldn't, didn't*).

Unfortunately—The sender is saying he or she has the power, and you don't. In an email, this word alerts me to something that's unpleasant and possibly insincere.

But—We all use this word too much. In business writing, it's too informal. The word *however* is not a good substitute. Use *and* instead.

Sincerely—It's meaningless as a go-to signature word.

Best—Be careful when you write this word in an email. Are your qualifications for the internship really the "best"? It is also another meaningless signature word, as you'll read later.

Interestingly—According to whom? Many times, the information that follows is "not that interesting."

Remotely—I'm guilty of this one. I tell my students and clients I'm working remotely, and that can mean I'm in another state or in a Starbucks two miles away. This word has lost its impact in the age of mobile computing so just say that you're offsite or off campus.

Avoiding buzzwords, clichés, jargon. Buzzwords are often derived from technical terms and are important sounding but lose their impact as many are used to impress others. They can be specialized terms or acronyms specific to an industry illustrating a common point or situation.

"Somewhat acceptable" buzzwords, jargon, and clichés can include: *actionable, back burner, bait and switch, bang for the buck, best practice, core competency, downsize, drilldown, gofer, hired guns, in the black, in the loop, level the playing field, leverage, lost in the sauce, low ball, out of pocket, organic, low hanging fruit, pushback, mom and pop organization, rubber check, silver bullet, skillset, stakeholders, take away, take this offline, traction, timeframe, value-added.*

Business jargon, clichés, buzzwords, and so forth can be good communication tools when inserted into a conversation appropriately, but what it really comes down to is using this terminology cautiously, infrequently, and at the right time.

Slang and cursing. Cursing is always a risk in business, especially for young professionals. You never know how you'll be perceived, and you shouldn't second guess your listeners by assuming cursing is not offensive to them.

Unfortunately, cursing and loose language is all too prevalent in business. We hear it used by professionals and superstars who should know better. Some use it as an attention-getter. It should never be used as the result of anger or to belittle someone, whether you're face to face, writing an email, or managing your Twitter account. As a member of the National Speakers Association and the International Federation of Speakers, I've taken an oath not to "curse" when giving a public presentation. So when I speak to an audience, I watch my words.

Power word examples. Here is a list of examples for you to reference in your business presentations, job interviews, and important meetings:

Management Power Words
Built
Demonstrated
Developed
Enhanced
Facilitated
Generated
Impacted
Implemented
Negotiated
Revitalized

Sales & Marketing Power Words
Closed

Collaborated
Delivered
Drove
Established
Generated
Increased
Presented

Prospected
Retained

Technical Power Words
Analyzed
Built
Consulted
Created
Escalated
Formatted
Integrated
Maintained
Programmed
Supported
Troubleshot

Academic Power Words
Applied
Authored
Counseled
Developed

Educated
Evaluated
Mentored
Nourished
Researched
Taught
Tutored

Healthcare Power Words
Assigned
Assessed
Assisted
Cared
Charged
Provided
Monitored
Nursed
Secured

Accounting Power Words
Analyzed
Audited

Justified
Verified
Prepared
Processed
Reported
Researched
Reviewed

Alphabetical List of Power Words

A
Abated
Abbreviated
Abolished
Abridged
Absolved
Absorbed
Accelerated
Acclimated
Accompanied
Accomplished
Achieved
Acquired
Acted
Activated
Actuated
Adapted
Added
Addressed
Adhered
Adjusted
Administered
Admitted
Adopted
Advanced
Advertised
Advised
Advocated
Affected

Aided
Aired
Allocated
Altered
Amended
Amplified
Analyzed
Answered
Anticipated
Applied
Appointed
Appraised
Approached
Approved
Arbitrated
Arranged
Articulated
Ascertained
Asked
Assembled
Assessed
Assigned
Assisted
Assumed
Attained
Attracted
Audited
Augmented
Authored
Authorized
Automated
Awarded

B
Balanced
Bargained
Benchmarked
Benefited
Bid

Billed
Blocked
Bolstered
Boosted
Borrowed
Bought
Branded
Bridged
Broadened
Brought
Budgeted
Built

C
Calculated
Canvassed
Captured
Cast
Cataloged
Catalogued
Categorized
Centralized
Chaired
Challenged
Changed
Channeled
Charted
Checked
Circulated
Clarified
Classified
Cleared
Coached
Co-authored
Collaborated
Collected
Combined
Commissioned
Committed

Communicated
Compiled
Completed
Complied
Composed
Computed
Conceived
Conceptualized
Condensed
Conducted
Conserved
Consolidated
Constructed
Consulted
Contributed
Controlled
Converted
Conveyed
Convinced
Coordinated
Corrected
Counseled
Created
Critiqued
Cultivated
Customized
Cut

D
Dealt
Debated
Debugged
Decentralized
Decreased
Deferred
Defined
Delivered
Demonstrated
Depreciated

Described
Designated
Designed
Detected
Determined
Developed
Devised
Diagnosed
Directed
Discovered
Dispatched
Dissembled
Distinguished
Distributed
Diversified
Divested
Doubled

E
Earned
Eased
Educated
Effected
Elicited
Eliminated
Emphasized
Enabled
Encouraged
Endorsed
Enforced
Engaged
Engineered
Enhanced
Enlarged
Enlisted
Enriched
Ensured
Established
Examined

Exceeded
Exchanged
Executed
Exempted
Expanded
Expedited
Explored
Exposed
Extended
Extracted

F
Fabricated
Facilitated
Fashioned
Fielded
Financed
Focused
Forecasted
Formalized
Formed
Formulated
Fortified
Founded
Fulfilled
Furnished
Furthered

G
Gained
Gathered
Gauged
Generated
Governed
Graded
Granted
Greeted
Grouped
Guided

H
Handled
Helped
Hired
Hosted

I
Identified
Illuminated
Illustrated
Implemented
Improved
Improvised
Inaugurated
Incorporated
Increased
Incurred
Individualized
Indoctrinated
Induced
Influenced
Initiated
Innovated
Inquired
Inspected
Inspired
Installed
Instigated
Instilled
Instituted
Instructed
Insured
Integrated
Interacted
Interpreted
Intervened
Interviewed
Introduced
Invented
Inventoried

Invested
Investigated
Invited
Involved
Isolated
Issued

J
Joined
Judged
Justified

K
Kept

L
Launched
Lectured
Led
Lightened
Liquidated
Litigated
Lobbied
Localized
Located
Logged

M
Maintained
Managed
Mapped
Marketed
Maximized
Measured
Mediated
Merchandised
Merged
Minimized
Modeled
Moderated

Modernized
Modified
Monitored
Motivated
Moved
Multiplied

N
Named
Narrated
Navigated
Negotiated
Netted
Noticed
Nurtured

O
Observed
Obtained
Offered
Opened
Operated
Orchestrated
Ordered
Organized
Oriented
Originated
Overhauled
Oversaw

P
Participated
Patterned
Performed
Persuaded
Phased
Photographed
Pinpointed
Pioneered
Placed

Planned
Polled
Prepared
Presented
Preserved
Presided
Prevented
Processed
Procured
Profiled
Programmed
Projected
Promoted
Prompted
Proposed
Proved
Provided
Publicized
Published
Purchased
Pursued

Q

Qualified
Quantified
Quoted

R

Raised
Ranked
Rated
Received
Recommended
Reconciled
Recorded
Recovered
Recruited
Rectified
Redesigned

Reduced
Refined
Regained
Registered
Regulated
Rehabilitated
Reinforced
Reinstated
Rejected
Remedied
Remodeled
Renegotiated
Reorganized
Repaired
Replaced
Reported
Represented
Researched
Resolved
Responded
Restored
Restructured
Resulted
Retained
Retrieved
Revamped
Revealed
Reversed
Reviewed
Revised
Revitalized
Rewarded

S

Safeguarded
Salvaged
Saved
Screened
Secured

Segmented
Selected
Separated
Served
Serviced
Settled
Shaped
Shortened
Shrank
Signed
Simplified
Simulated
Sold
Solicited
Solved
Spearheaded
Specialized
Specified
Speculated
Spoke
Spread
Stabilized
Staffed
Staged
Standardized
Steered
Stimulated
Strategize
Streamlined
Strengthened
Stressed
Structured
Studied
Submitted
Substantiated
Substituted
Suggested
Superseded
Supervised

Supplied
Supported
Surpassed
Surveyed
Synchronized
Systematized

T
Tabulated
Tailored
Targeted
Taught
Tightened
Took
Traced
Traded
Trained
Transacted
Transferred
Transformed
Translated
Transmitted
Transported

Treated
Tripled
Troubleshot
Tutored

U
Uncovered
Underlined
Underscored
Undertook
Underwrote
Unearthed
Unified
United
Updated
Upgraded
Urged
Used
Utilized

V
Validated
Valued

Verbalized
Verified
Viewed
Visited
Visualized
Voiced
Volunteered

W
Weathered
Weighed
Welcomed
Widened
Withstood
Witnessed
Won
Worked
Wrote

X-Z
Yielded

Technology Etiquette

INTRODUCTION: YOUR "E-PERSONALITY": AN ASSET OR A LIABILITY?

History repeats itself. Your grandparents or *their* parents were told not to listen to too much radio, your parents or grandparents were told not to watch too much TV, and you're told to put your phone down.

The business world today is dominated by e-communication. Emails and texts have replaced in-person meetings and phone calls. The good news is that it's quick. The bad news is that technology can encourage people to communicate with less empathy. One heated email can foster a string of other heated emails and suddenly, you've got a toxic work environment. People say things in an email or text that they would never say to someone's face. They post things on Facebook or Tweet commentary they would rather not deliver in person.

Is your e-personality a liability or an asset? Devices that enable you to do your job faster, across greater distances, reaching many people but with less human contact do <u>not</u> eliminate the need for *politeness*. If anything, inanimate objects like mobile devices *increase* the need for civility. Don't let bad behavior when sending an email, texting someone, or posting something online spill over to other professional situations. Just because you sit in front of a computer, tablet, or mobile device does not mean you can ignore etiquette without the consequences that may come later.

PLUGGED-IN POLITENESS RULES

Around 2008, the bottom fell out of the meetings industry. Sales meetings, annual conferences, and corporate retreats were being postponed or cancelled because of the economy. At that time, one of our valued clients—a large manufacturer with a global presence—cancelled their annual sales meeting. I was scheduled to conduct a workshop during that meeting, so obviously the cancellation impacted my bottom line.

Several months later, I had a conversation with the CEO who told me the meeting was being rescheduled for the following year, even though the economy had only slightly improved. He told me the decision to cancel last year's meeting was a mistake. He said that the opportunity for his sales teams to meet face to face regardless of the economy was of more value than the money he saved by canceling the meeting.

Face time will always be the most effective venue for business meetings and discussions, but it's not always possible to come face to face in terms of time and money. With many meetings being replaced by phone calls, texts, and emails, you should be aware of ways to keep your reputation *in tact with technology:*

1. **Know your environment.** Don't try to impress people with your use of technology if they're not as tech savvy as you. If your company insists on PowerPoint rather than Prezi, then go with PowerPoint. If company meetings mean phones off and away, then follow the protocol. Politely offer to assist others if you can, in learning new technology.

2. **Don't be a noise polluter.** Don't be the one who disturbs everyone in your office with your ringtone volume, or the one whose keypad sound drives others to the brink of delirium. Set your device to silent mode when you leave your desk or are at a meeting, and make sure you choose a silent ring tone. Go to a private place at least twelve feet away from others for personal conversations on your mobile device when you're in public.

3. **Turn your mobile device off and place it face down during a meeting, presentation, or other gathering.** This is a small gesture that communicates you value others at the meeting more than your device.

4. **Put your mobile device away during a job interview.** Don't even take your phone into the interview with you if you'll be tempted to steal glances at it, take calls, or check texts. Store it out of sight. Bring a pencil and paper instead. As one hiring manager put it, "Candidates who take calls during the job interview won't get one from us afterwards." Don't sit outside the interviewer's office waiting your turn while hunched over with your head buried in your phone or wearing headphones.

5. **Tell others when you need your phone.** If you are expecting a *very* important phone call (a family member is critically ill, for example) while at a meeting or job interview, say so <u>at the beginning</u> of the meeting. This is a simple gesture that gets the same response every time, which is, "That's no problem, thanks for letting us know."

6. **Tell others if you're using your phone for same-time business.** Using your phone to set reminders or make related notes is acceptable but tell others that's what you're doing so they know you're on task. *"I'll make a note to send you information on the presentation,"* is better than staring at your phone during the entire meeting.

7. **Talk your text.** It's okay to text when you're with someone but only if it's pertinent to your conversation. You might say, *"I'm sending a voice text to Beth right now to let her know about the change in our agenda."* Then put your phone away.

8. **Post only the positive.** Social media platforms are not the place to gripe about your boss or coworkers or express discontent with your current position. A subliminal message of an otherwise cute animal making a face with the caption, *"I hate Mondays...!"* can send the wrong message to your employer about how you regard your internship or position. Posting or reposting information regarding political or religious opinions could prove to be detrimental. I realize there's freedom of speech, but you need to make the decision of how *free* you want to be with your speech to maintain a level of respect and cooperation with coworkers and your boss, especially those you've "friended" on a social media platform. This type of open expression is risky when you're starting your career. Either abstain or find an employer who is not bothered by this type of public expression or an industry that encourages open commentary online.

9. **Don't be cryptic.** Not everyone understands text lingo or abbreviations. Send a complete message when you're sending business-related information and check your spelling and grammar. One student who wanted to meet with me after class sent this text request: *"Professor, I would like to sleep with you after class."* He forgot to check his spelling, and he was mortified with embarrassment the next time he came to class.

10. **Get real.** Record your voice mail in *your own voice.* When you're sending out applications for internships or jobs and you've provided your mobile phone number to a prospective employer, they'd rather hear your voice over the default recorded voice. During the job or internship application process, always answer your phone professionally. *"Hello, this is Lynne Breil."*

11. **Use headphones but use them politely.** Just because you're using headphones doesn't mean that we can't hear your music blaring through them. Headphones shouldn't be worn when you're waiting your turn for an internship or job interview, while you're attending a job fair, or in an environment where you're anticipating meeting and talking to others.

12. **Pick a ring tone that's not offensive.** When you're in the process of applying for an internship or job, it's probably a good time to reevaluate your ringtone. When in a professional environment, it's not funny to have a ring tone of a song with offensive language, and it's not cute if your ring tone was your favorite song when you were a freshman. Select something that offends no one and speaks of professionalism.

13. **Be selective with "selfies."** They're not always appropriate. When on vacation, go for it. When you're in a private business environment, a funeral, or a solemn event, selfies are not appropriate.

14. **Don't overuse hashtags.** While useful to discovering photographs, use them sparingly in your posts, tweets, and in other social media platforms.

THIRTY EMAIL TIPS FOR BUSINESS

"The future masters of technology will have to be lighthearted and intelligent. The machine easily masters the grim and dumb."
—MARSHALL McLUHAN

Email is going to be around for a long while. It's the most widely used form of communication in business, so all professionals should try to use email etiquette to improve their e-communication. Unfortunately, email can be a platform for rudeness, because people think they can say anything to anyone in an email.

Your **first impression email** to a hiring manager or potential client speaks volumes. A professional email is different than a personal email; and it should be. For one, you're trying to create a good impression to someone who you want to work for, and this someone is judging you in return. The average amount of time spent reading an email is about eleven seconds, according to a 2016 study. Make those eleven seconds count.

We recently compiled a program for a client who told us her managers weren't getting responses to their emails, or if they did, the response was incomplete or not clear. Of course, the managers blamed everyone but themselves on the problem when much of it was due to the way they wrote and formatted their emails. Enter, our thirty email tips for business. These tips will also work for you when communicating with hiring managers.

If you're not getting a response to your email, don't blame the recipient. The problem might be *you*.

WRITING AN EMAIL

1. **Respond** to your emails. I'm not talking about spam messages. It's difficult to reply to every message ever sent to you, but you should try, especially if the sender is expecting a reply (hiring managers, colleagues, other professionals). If you don't have the information they're asking for, send a *bridge email,* which is a short message saying that you'll be back in touch (give them the timeframe) when you're able to respond with appropriate information. In doing do, senders know you've received and read their email and you consider it important enough to respond. Don't give recipients opportunities to guess why you're not getting back to them.

2. Don't confuse **email** with **texting.** Text language, acronyms, and buzzwords can confuse recipients and make you look unprofessional. Stick to writing full words and use layperson's terms to get your point across. There are exceptions depending on who you're emailing. For example, certain acronyms or abbreviations may be acceptable when you're sending an email to someone who works in the same company.

3. Include a clear, direct relevant **subject line.** Thirty percent of the people you email will decide whether to open your email based on the subject line. Summarize the point of your communication and outline the reason for your message upfront, and you'll get a faster response. Here are some examples: "Report information from June meeting" rather than just "Report." "Agenda details for supervisor's meeting" rather than just "Agenda." Tagging an email as high priority or starting your subject line with "URGENT" is fine when absolutely necessary, which is maybe once in your career!

4. **Change** the [subject line] field when the conversation has moved off topic. Don't just find a previous email from that person and respond back without changing the subject line; you'll give the perception that you're lazy. Always start a new email and add contacts to your address book so you can add them with one click.

5. Use a professional **salutation.** "Yo" and "Hey" are not good choices. Use "Hi" or "Hello," followed by the person's name. Err on the side of formality (*"Hi, Mr. Bowman"*), especially if your new contact might be your parents' age or older. Most professional contacts

don't mind being called by their first names, but don't assume unless you know them. For group emails use a non-gender-specific term: *Managers, Participants, Project Team.* Get in the habit of using a salutation in every email unless you're communicating inside your organization with someone you know well.

6. Stick to **one subject** per email. It's easier for the reader to process, act upon, and respond back. Don't use an email to list ten things you want your coworkers to address. Clearly state your purpose and send a separate email if there's another issue, to ensure a quicker response.

7. Stay above the **scroll.** The ideal size for an email is **five to six sentences** or **150 to 200** words. In a recent survey by email marketing expert Sidekick, 39 percent of professionals consider long-winded emails to be their number one pet peeve. If you have that much information to share, organize a meeting.

8. **Proofread** every message. Proofread for grammar, spelling, and proper sentence structure. Don't rely on spell check. Remember, emails can be shared easily, and you want to communicate like you're an educated person. Don't be too lazy to check before you send. Your mistakes won't go unnoticed by the recipients of your email, and depending upon the recipient, you may be judged for making them.

9. Be cautious with **humor.** Years ago, there was a movie, *Lost in Translation,* which is exactly what happens with humor in an email without the right tone of voice or facial expression. When in doubt, leave it out. Something perceived as funny when spoken may come across differently when written. With that, limit the use of emoticons to *enhance* your humorous message. Many times, they do not appear on the recipient's email the same as the sender's and it adds to the confusion.

10. Use **exclamation points** sparingly. Try using only **one** exclamation point in an email. People sometimes get carried away with them. Multiple exclamation points can appear too emotional or immature.

11. Know that people from **other countries** speak and write differently. Globally people tend to be more formal, so don't use someone's first name or shorten their name (e.g., *Michael* to *Mike*). Writing an email to global partners is tricky because you can't see their body language. We will address this more in Chapter

5. Also remember that writing time zones requires the attached zone acronym (EST, PST, or "your time"); writing dates should be done this way, with the month written out: August 6, 2018, not 8/6/18.

12. Use a meaningful **closing**. Include your name, separate from your signature block. Keep your closing in line with your overall tone or to reflect the purpose of your email. Try these options: (a) Use a form of thanks *("Thanks for your help")*. (b) Use a call to action *("Get back to us if you have any questions")*. (c) End with a personal pleasantry *("Have a great vacation next week")*. Closings such as "Best," "Sincerely," and "Warm Regards" are meaningless in a business email.

13. Use a **signature block**. Your signature block is not your closing. (See above.) A signature block is meant to give your reader some information about you. I require my students to create a signature block for their emails. They're instructed to keep it to five to six lines and include the following:
    ✓ Name
    ✓ Position (major course of study along with anticipated graduation date)
    ✓ Company name (college or institution)
    ✓ Phone numbers (office and mobile)
    ✓ Email address and social media address(s)
    ✓ Website link (company, college, or institution; include the http:// so the URL is recognizable and an easy click-through)
    Use the same font, type size, and color as the rest of the email.

I have two signature blocks, a long one and a short one. I include a signature block on every email I send or reply to, with very few exceptions. I use the long version for introductory emails and when I'm first communicating with the person. I use the short version when there have been back-and-forth messages, or for *internal* email communication with my associates.

Here are examples:

A. THE LONG VERSION

Lynne Breil, CSP *(Certified Speaking Professional)* – Founder and CEO

The Professional Edge, Inc. York PA USA
http://www.theprofessionaledgeinc.com
Lynne@theprofessionaledgeinc.com
Author of the Upcoming Book:
Best in Class: Etiquette and People Skills for Your Career
Publisher: Kendall Hunt
Release date: Fall 2018
717 • 755 • 3333 (Office)
717 • 385 • 3041 (Mobile)

B. THE SHORT VERSION:

Lynne Breil, The Professional Edge, Inc.
York PA USA
http://www.theprofessionaledgeinc.com
Lynne@theprofessionaledgeinc.com
717 • 755 • 3333 (Office)
717 • 385 • 3041 (Mobile)

14. Use your **logo** in your signature block. *Make it **clickable.***
15. Keep tabs on your **tone.** You'd be surprised how many office workers say they've had confrontations with colleagues due to a misunderstanding over an email. Always write your email as if it's going to be read by everyone else in your organization, and keep it professional. Read your message aloud before hitting "send" to avoid misunderstandings. If it sounds harsh to you, it will sound harsh to the reader. Avoid using negative words, trigger words (as described in Chapter 1), and always say "please" and "thank you."

SENDING AN EMAIL

16. Avoid sending **one-liners.** This is the opposite of the "War and Peace" email and it is a pet peeve of many professionals. To make sure the recipient knows you've read the whole message, write a sentence instead of one word to avoid being misunderstood (*"I got your information and will attend the meeting"* instead of *"Yes"*).
17. Use your **professional** email address. Always use a professional email that conveys your name, so the recipient knows exactly who is sending the email. Email addresses I've seen from some students include *beerlover@..., babygirl@....* These convey more "party" than "professionalism."
18. Respond to all **questions** in an email. People will make up their own information if they don't get it from you. To control your information, make sure you answer all questions in an email, or send a *bridge email* as mentioned previously to let the sender know when you'll respond with more detail.
19. Avoid sending **heavy email attachments**. First, ask the recipient if it's okay to send the large file and ask if his or her system will support the software. Explore other options like file transfer tools or common locations (**SharePoint, Drop Box**) to upload heavy files and then share the URL of the location where the file has been uploaded. Avoid sending large files after hours, on weekends, or without warning to the recipient.
20. CC and **bcc** appropriately. Less is more when you **CC.** Before copying others on an email ask yourself, "Do they *all* need this information, or is there something they can add to the conversation?" Alternatively, not copying everyone whose name you mentioned in an email is like talking behind their back, so copy them.

The **bcc** feature allows you to copy someone without others knowing it and there are times when that may be a good idea, like:

- ✓ When contacts do not personally know each other
- ✓ When you've been asked to complete a task and include the requester via bcc
- ✓ When corresponding with an upset client or colleague and you want to let your boss or supervisor know (via bcc) he or she may be brought into the communication

21. Double check that you've selected the **correct recipient.** Add the email address last or delete the recipient's address and insert it last only when you're sure the message is ready to be sent. Sending an email to the wrong person will make you look unprofessional.

22. **Forward** an email purposefully. Don't be a habitual forwarder. Here are three rules to follow:

- ✓ Choose people you know will be interested; not everyone is.
- ✓ Include a personal comment on why you're forwarding the email to them (*"Anne, I thought you'd like this article on leadership from Forbes.com"*).
- ✓ Don't forward jokes and non-business-related email to another person's email address.

23. Keep email recipient's names **private.** How would you feel if your friends decided to take your phone number and give it out to strangers? When sending an email to multiple recipients (for example, announcing a new product for your internship company's best customers), put your address in the To: field and everyone else in the bcc: field to protect their email addresses. You can also search the Help tab or support website for your email software for information on the bcc.

24. Think twice before hitting **Reply All.** This is a common pet peeve, and no one wants to read emails from twenty people that have nothing to do with them. Ignoring these incoming emails is not always easy; many people get notifications on new messages or distracting pop-up messages on their screens to alert them. Think about who really needs to see your message, and don't bother the rest.

GENERAL EMAIL ETIQUETTE TIPS

25. **Size** matters. Use a 10- to 12-point type in an email.

26. Keep your **fonts** classic. Consider these screen-friendly fonts to give your emails an updated look: Verdana, Trebuchet MS, and the serif font, Georgia. (Serif fonts with all those little legs and tails create an impression of reading a book and give a more classy look. Sans serif fonts [those without serifs] give a cleaner, more modern look.) Avoid using red font or red color to denote or indicate a problem. Use uniform type, size, and color of font (black and blue are the best colors for email). Be careful of imbedded images; your email could be blocked as spammy or your recipients may not have their email program configured to support imbedded images and they could come through looking different. Bottom line: Your emails should be easy for other people to read.

27. Keep an eye on your **junk** or **spam** folder. Up to 70 percent of email traffic is spam. Content filters can be overzealous, so you need to frequent your junk folder with an eye toward subject fields or senders with names you recognize. Checking your spam filter is important if there are foreign emails with new domain names which might be blocked.

28. Switch off automatic **receipts.** Do not request read and delivery receipts unless your supervisor asks you to do so, and hopefully, there's a good reason. This is the feature that asks you to let the email sender know you have see his or her email. If you want to know if someone has received your email, pick up the phone.

29. **Read** all emails carefully. Use organizational features that allow you to "flag" or "categorize" your emails so you can come back to them later and not forget.

30. **Pick up the phone** for threads of more than three messages on the same topic. Do this more often. Since email is the most commonly used form of communication in business, it's open to interpretation and complexities that need to be explained in detail. When you have time-sensitive information that can be wrapped up with a phone chat instead of a lengthy thread of email communication, think how much more productive you'll be.

MATCHMAKING: MEDIUM TO THE MESSAGE

Email is more than just the transmission of information. It's also about managing a relationship remotely. Email is not a "one size fits all," meaning that it's not appropriate for *all* types of messages.

If you think there's room for misinterpretation of your message, select another medium like the telephone, a face-to-face meeting, or maybe a combination of the two as described here:

Email	<ul><li>Use for short, transaction-oriented messages that include precise numbers, well-formed concepts</li><li>Use to share insights you want people to be able to refer to later</li><li>Use to give friendly, upbeat information</li><li>Do not use to express negative information, argue, or criticize</li><li>Do not use to deliver bad news</li></ul>
Face-to-Face or Phone Meeting	<ul><li>Use for messages with high emotional content</li><li>Use to deliver negative or bad news</li><li>Use if you're not sure how the information will be received</li><li>Use for vague information</li><li>Use if something needs discussion</li></ul>
Email or Voicemail	<ul><li>Use to deliver good news</li><li>Use to deliver information that the receiver can save and refer to later with accuracy</li></ul>
Email and Phone Combined	<ul><li>Use for lengthy, complex, or detailed information where there may be attachments included</li><li>Use when a face-to-face discussion cannot be arranged</li></ul>

Email, along with other software communication that offers instant messages, group chatting, virtual meetings, productivity apps, and more, does not promise that those who use it will use it appropriately. People will be offended, conversations postponed, and productivity compromised. When you're using technology in business, think of the criteria Letitia Baldridge, author of *New Complete Guide to Executive Manners* (1995, one of the first books on the topic of business etiquette) used to determine guidelines for manners in business: *kindness, efficiency,* and *logic.* These three also are relevant applicators for e-communication.

MANNERS FOR MOBILE DEVICES

"Every once in a while a revolutionary product comes along that changes everything."

—STEVE JOBS

We are in the midst of a mobile takeover. Surprise! Since 2014, when the U.S. Consumer Device Preference Report showed that 65 percent of email was being accessed via mobile devices in the United States, email reading is shifting away from the desktop. Composing an email on a mobile phone is tricky, but there are some considerations you should consider:

- **Is your mobile device the best medium?** Reply from your desktop when you have a lot to say, or if what you have to say requires a lot of thought. For many, writing an important email is easier when you're sitting at your computer (e.g., answering a number of questions from a potential employer or internship coordinator).
- **Can you simplify your message for a mobile device?** Make sure that your email is short and straight to the point if you know the recipient will answer your email on a mobile device, **but don't be rude.** Do a quick review before you send your email to make sure that you're setting the right tone.
- **Did you turn off predictive text?** This avoids any embarrassing errors that could make you look stupid. (Predictive text is the input technology that facilitates typing on a mobile device by sug-

gesting words the end user can insert in a text field, based on the context of other words in the message and the first letters typed.)

- **Did you include a relevant subject line and salutation?** Don't leave the subject line blank or send an email that only consists of the text in a subject line. Salutations are important, too. A quick "Hi Tom" is better than launching right into your message.

- **Are you offensive with your camera?** Snapping a picture of colleagues during a social event, when they clearly prefer not to be photographed, is an example. Many people are particular about being tagged in photos that are not flattering. "Instragramming" food photos has received some very negative press lately, and restaurants have cracked down on people snapping pictures of their food because it is distracting for other diners.

- **Do you have an appropriate signature block?** Set an auto text that will appear at the end of each message (i.e., an abbreviated signature block) that includes at least your name, title, company, email, and phone. The mobile signature that reads *"Sent from my iPhone"* is not a complete signature block for a business email.

- **Can you shrink your links?** Clean up long hyperlinks on your phone. You can download a URL shrinker app like *bit.ly* to avoid bombarding recipients with long links that take up the whole mobile screen.

- **Did you double-check your message for typos?** Always check, but also consider setting a precondition text that appears at the *beginning* of a message. This would be something like, "Sent from my mobile phone. So sorry if the reply is brief." This will prepare the recipient for any typos, errors, or layout issues.

- **Is your message text language or email language?** Abbreviations can be a great tool and can save valuable time, but they can get lost in translation. Never think it's okay to communicate in text language just because ur (excuse me, *you're*) writing an email from your mobile device. For example, the once beloved LOL is becoming a bit old school in that nobody uses it anymore. But back in its heyday it confused older business people (including a manager we worked with a pharmaceutical company who thought it meant "lots of love"). This manager embarrassed his staff at a sales conference by eluding to the term incorrectly (as in "lots of love") throughout his presentation. The correct translation is *laughing out loud.*

> **PROFESSIONAL TEXTING ETIQUETTE:** Don't be a texting "lemming" (just because everyone else is doing it). Business texting should be used sparingly and should not be your primary form of communication. Don't even think of texting business associates unless they've texted you first or given you permission, and refrain from uninvited texting outside business hours. Keep your texts professional, avoiding acronyms and abbreviations. Do not mass text unless all parties have agreed to participate. Do not use texting to change meeting times/places/dates (not everyone may read the text in time). Respond to texts promptly and don't relay bad news via a text message. Last, don't be a digital stalker by calling, then emailing, then texting about the same subject you want an answer on—unless it's truly urgent.

YOUR ONLINE PRESENCE AND SOCIAL MEDIA

"Focus on how to be social, not on how to do social."

—Jay Baer

© Tashatuvango/Shutterstock.com

In a recent *Psychology Today* study, three of five people say someone is rude to them on social media more than once a month. The average

Facebook user has 130 friends (the average person knows 300 people by name, coincidentally), and more people log into Facebook than Google.

Even if you're not a Facebook user (and many of my students have opted for other social media platforms like Instagram, MySpace, Google+, FourSquare, or Pinterest), chances are your company will have a Facebook page. And that's good, because Facebook has an estimated 757 million users!

Don't be surprised if your internship duties include asking you to friend a million strangers and let them know about your company's new product or special event. I've seen it happen. In business, your brand exposure can be increased exponentially with social networking and many student interns are asked by their mentoring organizations to help with social media exposure. Today, that is likely to include the *online business trinity* of Facebook, LinkedIn, and Twitter.

One thing that holds true from an organizational perspective, after pouring over online comments about social networking, is that social media etiquette and social media policies need to be spelled out in a professional setting. New "rules" are being posted every day. Etiquette for e-social interactions will evolve from professionals who regularly and successfully use social media.

You might be a guru at social media platforms and communicating with friends through these applications, but in business you should adopt an observational mode, and seek out those professionals who know what they're doing before you e-communicate with business colleagues the same way you e-communicate with friends.

GENERAL SOCIAL NETWORKING PRACTICES

If the company you work or intern for is prolific with social media, no doubt they have a social media policy that spells out guidelines of engaging on behalf of the company.

To start, here are several social media policies for you or your company:

- **Understand the written and "unwritten" policies of conduct for your company's social network or digital collabo-**

ration space. If no rules are written, ask someone you trust, the HR managers, or your boss, *before* you take a chance.

- **Share your personal contact list wisely.** If you're interning in the sales department, for example, your company may request you to share networks internally because "it's what everybody else does." Ultimately, it's your personal choice.

- **Focus on productivity.** Professional social networking is meant to help others get things done; building contacts, retrieving information, accessing colleagues for help. Don't get too personal or too transparent by being "cute" or self-effacing over your company's digital channels. While you want to show your personality, it could make others feel uncomfortable. Post applicable, well-versed, and respectful content.

- **Redirect public and private information.** Rather than sending a message to an entire group, select niche recipients. Choose email or text for a private message eliciting an action or response.

- **Pass the "CEO Test."** Before posting, blogging, or messaging, ask yourself if you'd be comfortable sending the same information (as it is written) to your company's CEO, president, executive director, *or* general counsel.

- **Lock down your profile.** Follow the Facebook privacy settings for your public personal information to make sure you're not sharing anything outside your comfort zone in the workplace. Many a job opportunity has been lost because an employer found something in a person's social media site that was a "deal breaker." A helpful website is www.mashable.com since Facebook privacy settings are complicated and change regularly.

- **Attend to telephone and email first.** Important and complete messages are still sent through telephone and email. Don't get so wrapped up in social networking that you forget the availability of other more effective media for your business communication.

- **Identify yourself.** Do not create a link from your blog to your company's website without identifying yourself as a company intern or employee.

- **Use your own email address.** When registering on social networks, blogs, or other online tools utilized for personal use, use your own email address rather than your company email addresses.

Social Media Pitfalls in the Workplace

> *"What happens in Vegas stays in Vegas; what happens on Twitter stays on Google forever!"*
>
> —Jure Klepic

© Dean Drobot/Shutterstock.com

- **Commit to social media long term.** Embrace social media as part of your business day. Whether you're handling your company's Facebook page, your own LinkedIn profile, or your Twitter account, set aside some time every day to work on it.
- **Respond to comments on your company's Facebook page if you're handling the posts.** Respond to as many as you can so they know you're there.
- **Decline requests by clicking "Ignore."** You shouldn't feel pressured if someone from your work sends you a "friend" request and you'd rather not accept.
- **Think twice before "friending" your boss.** Most bosses and supervisors feel uncomfortable when they get "friend" requests from their direct reports. If you do connect, utilize privacy settings and different friend lists to control how you share content.

- **Include a photo.** I've seen everything from alpacas to abstract drawings instead of a picture. Your photo confirms that you're the right person. Make sure your image is professional looking. Choose a current professional photograph if you can. Otherwise, select a clear picture of you looking directly at the camera and smiling. Don't select a photo where you're standing next to someone at your cousins' wedding reception that includes a fourth of their shoulder and the DJ in the background. Include your photo on your Twitter account as well.
- **Ask before you tag.** This is especially important in business. Check your own photos periodically to make sure you haven't been tagged in an embarrassing or uncompromising photo. Pay attention to social media alerts (Facebook, Instragram, Twitter) that appear any time you've been tagged in a photo.
- **Complete your LinkedIn profile.** LinkedIn, the headhunter you never knew you had, has a few superb applications that can help you build your "personal brand." It's a clever job-hunting ploy and nearly every industry uses LinkedIn to find and vet job candidates. Over 90 percent of recruiters rely on the site, according to data from the Society of Human Resource Management.

  Many of my students send me their profiles and ask me to connect with them on LinkedIn after graduation. In doing this, they're making it easy for me to refer them to a potential employer. Get a head start now and build your LinkedIn profile so you can catch an employer's eye, make business connections, and join professional LinkedIn groups.

TELEPHONE AND VOICEMAIL

> *"Be a master of your phone, not a slave to it."*
> —EMILY POST

Another assignment I give my students, in addition to creating a signature block, is to record their voicemail in their own voice.

Several years ago, I had an opportunity to work with a large law firm in central Pennsylvania. They asked me to do a program on professional etiquette. I talked to the HR manager beforehand to find out more about the firm and what their issues were. One of them, she told me, was the voicemail message of one of the partners, who had his paralegal record this message for him: "Attorney [his name] does not respond to voicemail. Please email him instead."

Clients and colleagues were offended, for two reasons. First, the email was less than accommodating to callers. Secondly, it was not recorded in the attorney's voice; he had his paralegal record it for him which might suggest to callers the task was beneath him.

Recording Your Voicemail Message

There is no impact that compares to delivering a clear, concise, professional message through your own unique human voice.

Below are recommended voicemail scripts for your phone. This is what your callers hear when they call and you're not available to answer. If you're applying for internships or job opportunities, this could be the first impression the hiring manager has of you.

Before you record your voice mail:

- Stand up and smile when you speak; you will sound more confident.
- Avoid background noise; you want to sound professional.
- Don't rush; enunciate clearly and speak slowly.
- Try to project a business tone.
- Rerecord until you're satisfied with the way you sound.

Voicemail script example that provides basic information:

"Hello, you've reached the voicemail of [your name, your title].

I'm [away from my desk, not available, in class] right now.

Please leave your name, telephone number, a short message,

and the best time to call you back.

I'll do my best to get back to you at that time.

Thanks for your call."

Voicemail script example that indicates you're away for an extended time:

"Hello, you've reached the voicemail of [your name, your title].

I will be unavailable from [date or time you'll be away]

to [date or time you'll be back].

Please leave a brief message with your contact information.

I'll call you back when I return.

Please reach [name of colleague/supervisor], [job, title] at [phone]

if you need to speak to someone before I return."

There are more creative messages out there, certainly. Some include quotes, business tips of the day, a motivational or inspiring thought, along with an unconventional way to introduce yourself at the beginning of the voicemail. *"Congratulations! You've reached the right person! Unfortunately, you've called at the wrong time...."*

I would caution young professionals and interns from creating catchy voicemail messages unless you've gotten full approval from your supervisor. Don't try to get "cute" or interject humor with your voicemail as you never know how hiring managers might perceive the message, especially if they haven't yet met you face to face.

Leaving a Professional Voicemail Message

You may think that most professionals today opt for email or texting, so it's not necessary to be prepared to leave a voicemail message. Whether you're using a landline or your mobile phone, leaving a professional voicemail is important for several reasons.

Many professionals deliberately let their calls go to voicemail so that they can check the caller ID and prioritize when they will return calls. Some offices train their staff *not* to take calls during meetings or during certain times of the day, so your call will go directly to voicemail. Last, not every person in a high position has an administrative assistant. They're answering their own calls and may not be able to pick up the phone when you call. You should always be prepared to leave a voicemail.

Before you leave a voicemail message:

- Jot down your key message points before you call.
- Don't leave your message from a noisy environment (the Bluetooth system in your car might not be the best).
- Smile and speak slowly. Write your phone number in the air as you say it to ensure that you're not speaking too fast.
  - Speak the last four digits in your phone number as: "thirty-one forty-eight, for "3148." This makes it easier to remember.
- Say your name/company/number at the <u>beginning and end</u> of message.
- State the purpose of your call.
- Tell the person when they can call you back; this avoids telephone tag.
- Be brief; your voice mail message should be thirty seconds or less.

A "TIME TESTED" VOICEMAIL SCRIPT

"Hello, this is [your name] with [your company/school] at [your phone].

It's [today's date] at [the time you're calling].

I'm calling about: [give one or two things].

You can call me back between [hours they can reach you]

or We need/I'd like to hear from you by 4:00 P.M. today.

Again, [your name] with [your company] at [your phone]."

COMMUNICATION, TECHNOLOGY, AND THE PLATINUM RULE

Age often dictates which technology one will use on the job. You'll see a difference in the channels used by your Baby Boomer CEO, your Gen-X supervisor, and your Millennial project coordinator.

I went to my freshman year in college with an electric typewriter and thought I was the "toast of the town" or rather, the dorm. Now, I've embraced all things e-communication to stay in sync with my students, colleagues, clients, and family.

There's a high learning curve to using electronic hardware, software, and all associated applications. You're not expected to know *everything,* but you will be expected to know a lot. Whatever technology you're given in your internship or job—and this includes that 140-year-old hunk of technology known as the telephone—know how to use it. Learn how to transfer calls with the same proficiency as you would access Google for information, go to Amazon.com to buy something, or sign into YouTube to learn how to do something.

More importantly, remember that generational differences influence e-communication styles. While you may be used to speed and brevity over grammar and spelling, your Gen-Xer boss may regard careless writing as a sign of incompetence.

Be mindful of generational differences, but ultimately choose the technology that best suits the people you're trying to reach. It's like the *platinum rule* of treating others how they would like to be treated.

chapter 3

General Workplace Etiquette

> *"If you say a bad thing,*
> *you may soon hear a worse thing said about you."*
>
> —HESIOD

There will be sticky situations in your internship and your job, just like the situation with the roommate you couldn't stand or the professor who treated you harshly. People will be rude to you. Not everyone will like you. Professionals have been saying that rudeness is "on the rise" for twenty-five years!

It's simple: Offend as few people as possible and make comfortable as many people as possible. Well, maybe not *that* simple. There will be times when you're not sure what to do or say. This chapter—just like the others—is designed to give you guidelines and insight into some frequently encountered "sticky" situations in the workplace.

CUBICLE AND SHARED SPACE ETIQUETTE

by Christina Butler, Media Communication Consultant and Training Associate, The Professional Edge, Inc.

SHARED SPACES

When I pictured my future career as a journalist as I was about to enter the news business, I visualized a state-of-the-art newsroom, with orderly files and flow, glamourous makeup rooms, and most excitingly: my own office. HA!

That's not how TV news works. The first real newsroom I walked into was a basement. It was dark, smelled like a flooded cellar, and had three burned out overhead lightbulbs. The makeup room was little more than a mirror that sat on your desk. And speaking of desks—they were everywhere—with no private work areas. Each employee from intern to main anchor had the same type of desk in the same open space.

While most offices are much cleaner than your typical newsroom, and hopefully have a maximum of one missing overhead lightbulb, data shows us about 70 percent of businesses with physical offices include some type of "open space" work stations.

This means there's a good chance that early in your career you will find yourself sharing an open space with your colleagues with not even a partition to divide you. (Although cubicles are popular, too, and they offer a bit more privacy. We'll discuss those coming up after the break. Sorry, I mean after *this*. I slipped back into reporter mode there.)

Why do employers choose an open space layout? For one thing, it's easy to communicate with others. Other reasons include: there's no visible hierarchy, it's cost effective, and space is maximized. Open spaces also allow for flexibility and impromptu meetings.

While an open space office layout lends itself to free-flowing conversation, if you want to get any work done it's important to set some limitations. Just because you can talk all you want to the person sitting next to you, doesn't mean you should. When you need to get down to business, consider some of these tips to establish ground rules with yourself and coworkers.

- **Have a signal**: Put a sign or piece of paper on top of your computer and let your coworkers know this means you are "in the zone."
- **Adopt an "adult study hall"**: Suggest an hour of the workday be "quiet time" for your immediate work area.
- **Give warning**: If you have an important phone call or project pop up, communicate that to your colleagues. They'll appreciate your heads up and likely respect your wishes for a few quiet minutes.

An open space desk also means anyone can see how you choose to keep your desk area tidy and decorated. About five years into my career, I was assigned a desk in the newsroom next to a very bright, friendly woman. A very bright, friendly woman who LOVED animal print and glitter. One picture frame or coffee mug would have sufficed, but this woman took it to a whole new level. Here we were—television news journalists talking about homicides and city bankruptcies—and there was an oversized glittering gold and cheetah-print painted wine glass sculpture bartering for our attention.

Work can become a home away from home, but that doesn't mean you need to have the same decorating standards in both places. You may love your gallery wall of concert tickets, spring break pictures, and beer signs in your dorm, home, or apartment, but they don't belong at work.

When it comes to your open space desk decorating, keep it professional. Here are some suggestions:

- Have no more than one or two regular sized picture frames with appropriate photos.
- Limit yourself to one mug if you crave caffeine. This forces you to continuously clean it and not leave around a collection of would-be science experiments.
- Keep the political, religious, or otherwise divisive decorations or statements at home. You have no way of knowing how your co-workers voted in the last election, and unless you have a very specific politically focused job, they shouldn't know your political feelings either.
- Have sanitizer available always. It's the one thing you should keep on your open space desk. Multiple studies show that employees in an open work space need at least three extra sick days per year than a closed-office setting employee.

Unlike the inside of a germ-infested newsroom, there are *some* things you should keep from spreading like your overly loud voice, medical history, eating and shopping habits. Read on to see how the rules of cubicle life can also help you survive and thrive in an "open space" workplace.

LIFE ON THE CUBE FARM

Somewhere between your graduation day and the day you find yourself sitting in the corner office as the one in charge, you'll likely end up in a cubicle.

A cubicle, by definition, is a small partitioned space. The average size hovers at six square feet, maybe eight square feet if you are lucky. Don't let the plot size scare you, though.

I've worked nearly every position in the television newsroom from assignment manager to anchor. For fifteen years, my office was the inside of a news van when I wasn't in the newsroom. That's not a lot of square footage, and even less when you consider there was also another human, a camera, a tripod, editing gear and computers, a chair, lighting equipment, curling irons, makeup, and leftover lunch remnants from the crew who used the van yesterday. (At least we pretended it was just from yesterday. One rudely scorching hot August day, the discovery of a month-old tuna fish sandwich squashed in a corner almost led to breaking news from right inside our van. The smell was that bad, I swear.)

It was hard to work at times, with a light pole digging in your side as you tried to write the day's top story. Of course, we always got it done. But the glory of a cubicle is, you don't have to have all that extra stuff! There's plenty of room to get your job done effectively. A standard cubicle is outfitted with a desk, computer or laptop, and a chair. Compared to a cramped live truck, that's real estate gold! The trick to capitalizing on that prime property is to know your boundaries and not to overdo it. Remember the colleague with the blinged-out desk? Her bedazzling wasn't dazzling to any of us, and your cubicle should follow the same golden rule: professionalism first. Let's talk basics.

People can see everything you are doing. It's the business blessing and curse of the cube. Need some quick input on a pitch you are about to make to a big client? Speak slightly above a whisper, and your neighbor can provide instant feedback. Want to check out how your colleague's Excel file is running new numbers? Just turn around or crane your neck around the corner.

Remember, people can see everything you are doing. This also means they can see if you are scouring Amazon Prime Day's top deals instead of working on the presentation due tomorrow. There were many days and long nights inside a live truck where I wanted nothing more than to stretch my legs up on the dash and recline my seat, but how would that look to anyone walking by our truck? It certainly wouldn't look like I was the one they should tune into at 11 p.m. because I'd been working hard all day to get the story right. Similarly, while you want to be comfortable in your office chair for eight hours a day, no colleague (or boss!) will get the impression you are working hard if you are reclined with your feet on the desk.

If they can see you, they can hear you. My husband spent the first ten years of his career as a project manager and sourcing specialist at a company where he had a large private office all to himself. He could blare conference calls, play videos from clients at full volume, and block out all distractions by simply shutting his door. When a new job and challenge enticed him away from that company, he suddenly found himself in a cubicle style office. "The quiet is piercing—until it's suddenly not there!" That's how I remember him describing his first few days. What he meant was, he could hear everything. Cubicles lend themselves to semi privacy; but you are still in an open setting. At its quietest, a keystroke, phone beep, or cough can be heard 'round the cube. At its loudest, that keystroke is drowned out by your colleague's side of a phone conversation closing a business deal or the watercooler hysterics reenacting the Christmas party dance-off competition.

THE TOP CUBICLE PET PEEVES

1. **Noise.** The most annoying noises include computer volume (see below: headphones will save you); speaker phone—arrange for a meeting room or private area if you're going to be on a conference call or on a speaker phone; talking to yourself; singing or humming (if you had a voice worthy of an audience, you wouldn't be working in a cubicle); talking to neighbors through cubicles, unless it is necessary. Even then, keep it brief. If it's worthy of a conversation walk the few steps to their cube.

Beyond your audio awareness, there are other things to steer away from in the land of cubicles. The following will ensure your colleagues are not sitting in their own cube plotting your forced departure.

2. **Food smells.** Don't be the eater. If you must eat at your desk, choose a meal that is not hot and does not make a lot of noise unwrapping. Those French fries and foil-wrapped burger may hit the spot for you, but your neighbor may be starving while trying to concentrate on meeting a deadline.

3. **Don't over share your life.** Your entire floor does not need to know about your upcoming doctor's appointment. Step outside for personal phone calls.
4. **Don't let your work area be a mess.** Yes, it offers more privacy than a completely open floor plan, but anyone walking by can still see the cleanliness (or lack of) in your cube.
5. **Don't sneak up on people.** Always announce yourself first or find a hard surface to knock on to let them know you have entered their space. Not everyone will be as cube-savvy as you and have an "entrance detector." Keep reading for that tidbit!

Surviving Cube Chaos and Commotion with Proper Etiquette

For all the challenges you may feel up against when you are new to the cubicle setting, there are ways to survive. Following are some tips from workers who have learned to make their semi-open space work for them.

A strategically placed mirror will let you know when someone is behind you. Most cubicle setups have your back to the opening of your space. You might find it easier to fully focus on the job (or computer screen) in front of you if you aren't constantly worried someone is looking over your shoulder or about to startle you.

Earphones save lives! A tad dramatic, perhaps, but my husband and other cube dwellers might argue it's not. They are a win-win. Use them to listen in on conference calls or videos without disrupting your neighbors; and abuse them by plugging them in to drown out the neighbor who keeps cackling at her sister-in-law's text messages.

Have a go-to plan for important meetings or phone calls. It is never okay to bring a client into your cubicle when there is the option of a private space you can use. Many offices will have at least one room that is available for such instances. Make sure you know how to secure it.

When you abide by the common courtesy guidelines of a cubicle, you can be a competent worker who does not add stress to your coworker's daily routines. And let's not forget that a cubicle has its pros!

- It's easier to meet new people and interface with colleagues.

- There's creative energy when people not only share a common goal, but a common physical location.
- You won't feel left out of conversations that surround workplace topics.
- It's budget friendly for an organization.

Now that you have cube etiquette down pat, you can focus 100 percent on your work. After all, you are in a cubicle because you have a job to do. Pay more attention to that than the attention others are paying to you, and your perfectly polished cube behavior will prevail. Do all of this, and sooner than later you may be able to swap those partitioned walls for real ones in your own office.

MEETING ETIQUETTE

One of the projects I assign my Business Communications class is to work as a five- to seven-person team on a case study and then give a group presentation to the rest of the class. In my mind, the project requires face-to-face and a few virtual meetings, but some of my students would rather "google doc" their way through the entire project than meet face to face because of bad experiences they've had working with others. There's nothing wrong with Google Docs; it's a way to bring and keep everyone on board during a group project. But, it cannot be

© nd3000/Shutterstock.com

the *only* way team members communicate especially when they have opportunities to meet together in the same room.

In your classes, internships, and in your first job you'll be expected to attend face-to-face meetings. Some will be productive and rewarding; others will be a waste of your time. This portion of the chapter is devoted to giving you meeting etiquette guidelines for preparation and participation. So if you want an "A" on your next group project, keep reading.

Do You Need a Meeting?

For my students to work on a case study and prepare for a group presentation, they know they need to meet as a group to get the job done. But, is a meeting always necessary?

Recently, a professional group I belong to was in crisis. Within two months, the vice chair resigned, and the chair moved to another city and another position. Right after the chair announced her impending move, a member of the advisory council called me and wanted to talk offline about the future of the organization. "What do you think we should do?" she asked. "We need to call a meeting," I replied. This situation perfectly fit the criteria for needing a meeting.

If you can answer "yes" to *any* of the following questions, you should call a meeting:

❏ Is there a *goal* for the meeting? (*What* do you want/need to do?)
❏ Is there a *purpose* for the meeting? (*Why* do you need to meet?)

In the case of my professional group, we broke down the goal and purpose this way: Discuss how to proceed without a chair and vice chair (*purpose of the meeting*); Put a short-term process in place (*goal of the meeting*).

❏ Is the job beyond the capacity of one person? (Does it require more time, effort, and information than one person has?)
❏ Are individuals' tasks interdependent? (Do people need to interact with each other to get things done?)
❏ Is there more than one decision or solution? (If there's only one decision or one way to proceed, there's no need for a meeting.)
❏ Are misunderstandings or reservations likely?

- ❑ Will the appropriate people be there? (If you can't bring together the right people, it's better to hold off the meeting until the right people can be in the room.)
- ❑ Has an agenda been created ahead of time? (Having an agenda ahead of time gives participants an opportunity to prepare and also helps you stay on task within the allotted time.)

Here is a sample meeting agenda. Many professionals we work with have this template downloaded on their PCs. They say their colleagues thank them for the clarity and time order.

SAMPLE MEETING AGENDA

Marketing Team Advisory Group

MEETING TIME: Friday, April 7 – 1-2 PM

LOCATION: First Floor Meeting Room

ATTENDEES: Thomas, Beth, Paige, Kathy, Barry, Aileen, Shelly

MEETING PURPOSE: To generate new ideas for marketing our upcoming corporate events

SCHEDULE:

8:00-8:05 Explain purpose; Review agenda, and "ground rules"

8:05-8:15 Reports
- Community appreciation event (Thomas)
- Budget (Beth)

8:15-8:35 Unfinished business
- Website redesign (2 design options will be presented – Paige)

8:35-8:45 New business
- Employee rewards (Kathy) Please bring ideas for what your department needs to know about new ways to reward employees.

8:45-8:55 Q and A

8:55-9:00 Next steps and assignments for follow-up

9:00 Adjourn

MEETING ETIQUETTE TIPS

We asked a group of supervisors from an organization with over 1,300 employees how they think their internal meetings could be improved. Some of their answers were:

- *Set objectives and goals prior to the meeting*
- *Arrive on time*
- *Have an opening activity that breaks the ice*
- *Eliminate distractions*
- *Have the right people there*
- *Allow time at the end for feedback*
- *Keep unrelated individual problems out of the meeting discussion*
- *Have the facilitator ask questions to the group to keep them engaged and help them understand processes and procedures*
- *Set ground rules at the beginning*

Their input was important and served as a baseline for the meeting etiquette tips we describe next. These suggestions are for students, interns, new hires, and "seasoned" professionals (who may need a refresher):

Before the Meeting:

- **Send out an agenda if you are leading the meeting.** Include the purpose or goal of the meeting. You'll read below that you can always *suggest* or help to *prepare* an agenda for your boss who's running the meeting.
- **RSVP if required.** Whether you confirm through an online poll or respond with an email or text, a confirmation shows that you're dependable and allows you to make a note of any logistics you'll need for the meeting. Use this opportunity to mention that you'll be late or need to leave early. Don't wait until the meeting begins to tell others about your early departure or late arrival.
- **Don't hog meeting space.** Block the room for your meeting but don't block out a room for days on end or turn the room into your personal office.
- **Be prepared to say something.** The outcome of a meeting will be the result of the quality of participation from attendees. Research, read, and bring any necessary materials with you that you'd like to share.
- **Bring a writing utensil and notepad.** These are not always provided; and recording notes on your digital device is many

times misread as if you're not paying attention. Don't show others you're a "meeting rookie" by asking for a pen and paper.

Upon Arrival:

- **Arrive on time!** On time means five to ten minutes early. This will show your commitment to the project and your participation.
- **Network before the meeting.** Sometimes people will gather at the coffee and doughnut table in the back of the room before the meeting starts. Use this opportunity to greet others, introduce yourself if you don't know someone, exchange business cards, and grab a cup of coffee before the meeting begins.
- **Ask where you should sit.** The person leading the meeting may dictate where people should sit, depending on his or her hierarchy. In more casual meetings, it's still a good idea to ask (especially if you're the "newbie") since there may be a seating precedence that you don't want to upset. If there's no particular seating protocol and you want to speak up during the meeting, take a seat where everyone can see and hear you, usually close to the person who's leading the meeting.
- **Make a cheat sheet.** When you're at a meeting with new people, you can impress them by remembering their names. When you first sit down, jot people's names in the same order which they are seated on a piece of paper or use the bottom of your agenda. If you can't remember someone, skip a space for that person and fill it in if you discover the name later in the meeting.
- **Set ground rules if you're leading the meeting.** Ground rules are special rules agreed upon by the participants or specified by the meeting leader that spell out procedures and what behavior is acceptable (positive) or not acceptable (negative) during the meeting.

Examples are:

"GROUND RULES" FOR A MEETING

- Arrive on time for meetings.
- Honor your assigned meeting preparation tasks or action items.
- Speak up if you have a question or disagree.
- Don't discuss disagreements behind others' backs.
- Give the meeting organizer no less than a 24 hour notice if you're going to miss the meeting.
- Don't talk over others; wait your turn.
- Ask for clarification if you don't understand something.

Participating in the Meeting:

- **Ask to be put on the agenda.** There's nothing wrong with asking if you can give an update on that project you've been working on, especially if your assignment will benefit the group. Share the sample agenda (above) with your boss, or create one for him or her with you on the agenda. Offer to print out the agenda for your boss as the meeting nears. Remember to take a seat close to the meeting leader if you want to be seen and heard.
- **Think before you speak.** Observe what's going on around you. Make a few notes about what you want to say *before* you open your mouth.
- **Raise your hand.** If you're *not* on the agenda, but it's your project, speak up. If that fails, you can always stand up.
- **Watch your body language.** Look at *everyone* when you speak, not just the person who asked you a question. Use the 75/25 rule: look at the questioner 25 percent of the time and the rest of the group 75 percent of the time when answering a question. Also, smile (it relaxes people) and keep your hands visible and on top of the table, not in your lap.
- **Listen first, take notes second.** People will be more impressed by your good listening skills than they will be by your taking copious notes. **Good listening skills** include making eye contact with the speaker, paraphrasing what they said, and asking clarifying questions. You're no longer in class and you don't have to impress the professor by acting like the court stenographer.
- **Don't linger.** Vacate meeting space promptly especially if others are waiting to use the room.
- **Tidy up.** Leave the space as you would wish to find it. Many years ago, I presented a workshop at a client location and forgot to remove a couple of easel pad pages on the walls. They were not happy and complained to my direct contact. Today, I never leave a meeting room without it being in pristine shape.

DIVERSITY, RELIGION, AND POLITICS IN THE WORKPLACE

"Inclusion is…integration beyond acceptance."
—UNKNOWN

DIVERSITY

As global markets emerge and grow, workplace diversity is nowadays a business necessity instead of a company's *gold star* to show that they're committed to embracing differences and change. A diversity of voices can broaden outlooks and improve discussions and decision making. Traditional diversity is a *given*.

Traditional diversity in the workplace means the inclusion of different races, ethnicities, gender identifiers, generations, and social classes. To many younger professionals, diversity also means differences in ideas, thoughts, philosophies, and skill sets. When diverse people, regardless of job title or years of experience, work together to solve problems and come up with new ideas, it forms bonds and makes for a better team.

As an intern or new hire, ask yourself where your workplace stands on diversity. Do people in your office think differently? Do they approach problems differently? Are they proficient at different things? It goes without saying that everyone should be treated fairly and given equal opportunity.

Organizations today know that Millennial workers desire inclusive work environments and want to contribute to them.

Here are some ways to help your organization create and sustain inclusive work cultures so they can recruit, attract, and hire the next largest workforce:

- Suggest that people work in face-to-face groups to complete mundane tasks, not in isolation.
- Suggest regular brainstorming sessions to foster innovation and creative thinking.
- Talk to others about what you could be doing differently to get your team working more like a team.
- Pitch in when there's a deadline to get things done; no task should be too small or below your paygrade.
- Accommodate to people with disabilities (e.g., place yourself at eye level when communicating with someone in a wheelchair).
- Talk to your boss, supervisor, or an HR manager if you see any form of discrimination at your work. (A chief reputation strategist for Weber Shandwick said that 69 percent of employed Millennials have seen or heard something related to discrimination at work.)
- Listen with the purpose of understanding, not waiting for your turn to talk.
- Ask questions if discussions make you uncomfortable or if they are confusing.

RELIGION AND POLITICS IN THE WORKPLACE

Religion is one of the subjects that can make for bad workplace conversations. (Others include politics, your sex life, problems with family members, and your health.)

Faith is a very personal thing about which people are very sensitive. You don't have to hide your religion, and you can mention things you do to celebrate it, but realize that not everyone worships the same way as you do.

In fact, one of the stories I use to illustrate that nervousness in public speaking is centuries old, is from the First Testament in the Bible. It's about Moses, and how God asks Moses to talk to the Israelites and get them to follow him out of Egypt. Moses pleads with God, telling him that he (Moses) is not good at [public] speaking; that his words do not come out of his mouth the right way when he speaks in front of a group of people. He ultimately tells God to go pick someone else. God argues back to Moses, reminding him who made his mouth and tongue and will give him the ability to find the right words. If you've read the Bible, you know the rest of the story. God wins, and Moses leads the Israelites out of Egypt.

I've used that story numerous times and have never once gotten any negative feedback. That's because I did not use the opportunity to speak positively or negatively about other religious practices, or others' beliefs.

Discussions on religion. Several years ago, a government client of ours reached out with a problem among their administrative staff in a large department. One of the administrators was inviting her co-workers—and using company time to extend the invite—to her church services. She was relentless in her attempts to get coworkers to come with her on Sunday morning and openly talked about her religion with anyone who would listen.

Many of the staff were offended and complained to the supervisor. They said their coworker was a "nice enough person," but now had created an uncomfortable workplace that was previously warm and welcome. She overstepped her boundaries when she tried to convert her coworkers to her faith.

Religious discussions can take place everywhere, from the sports field to the break room. But you should be very cautious about joining a religious discussion in the workplace, especially if you're new to the company.

Here are some tips to avoid uncomfortable or unwelcome discussions about religion.

- Talk about things you do to celebrate your religion, if asked. You don't have to hide it.
- Keep negative opinions you might have about others' beliefs or lack of religious affiliation to yourself.
- Don't persuade anyone to convert to your faith.
- Be direct if a coworker tries to convert you to his/her faith: *"Thanks so much for your concerns about me, but I'm fine and don't need spiritual advice right now."*

- Ask your supervisor to step in and handle the situation if it is making others feel uncomfortable. For example, you might suggest that your supervisor address the topic in an upcoming department meeting, or let the company president or CEO write a message in the next newsletter dictating what's acceptable or unacceptable regarding these types of discussions in your organization.

Discussions on politics. Politics can be a highly volatile topic. It causes people to do and say things that end relationships. And because you're at work forty-plus hours a week, you need to get along with your coworkers. Engaging in political discussions is probably not worth it, even in an election year.

My oldest son is a news anchor in a city with a large viewership, and he's reported on numerous regional, statewide, and national elections. It goes without saying that his viewers will never know his political views, but he also has a good rule of thumb when it comes to sharing political views with coworkers. He assumes that everyone around him is of the opposite party. He plans his political comments accordingly, even when he gets together with coworkers after hours.

Here are some tips to avoid uncomfortable or unwelcome discussions about politics:

- Do not try to win your coworkers over to your side.
- Check your company's policy on wearing political clothing or bringing campaign materials into the workplace; many offices have guidelines.
- Don't use work time to tweet or blog your political views.
- Approach any political discussion as a conversation, not a debate. Example: *"What do you think about Bernie Sanders? I know you follow politics and I'm wondering what your thoughts are."*
- Stay away from hot button issues like same-sex marriage and abortion.
- Walk away when things get heated. Example: *"I need to get back to my desk for a 1:00 phone call before lunch is over."* Or *"This conversation is getting a little too heated for the office—can we agree to disagree and change the subject?"*
- Save your campaigning for the weekend.

chapter 4

Business Social Events and the Business Meal

> *"The world was my oyster, but I used the wrong fork."*
> —OSCAR WILDE

INTRODUCTION: THE PURPOSE OF THE BUSINESS MEAL

The business meal *is* a time-honored way to cultivate business relationships and close business deals. Each meal meeting is an opportunity for relationship building. **The purpose of the business meal is business.**

When you join colleagues, potential employers, or other industry professionals at a meal, you're opening an opportunity to sell yourself or sell something (an idea, product, etc.). Unfortunately, 40 percent of us prefer to "brown bag" it, according to a recent restaurant trade association survey. When you're invited to join others for a *business lunch*, take advantage of the opportunity to "break bread" with them.

We've all learned dining rules from childhood, like keeping your elbows off the table or not talking with food in your mouth. In this chapter, you'll learn some new rules about the business meal, in an A to Z format. I've also included tips on how to eat difficult foods (probably *not* what you'd order on a job interview meal). If they are (not by your choice) put in front of you, you won't make a fool of yourself.

HOW BUSINESS DINING IS DIFFERENT

- In business, **the focus is on building the relationship**; food is secondary. Meal meetings are purposeful opportunities to network. For example, sending food back to the kitchen when it's not prepared to your liking interrupts the flow of the meal.
- In business, **keeping the same eating pace as your dining partner is important** and shows your adaptability and flexibility.
- In business, **small-talk topics should be carefully considered** and the transition from small talk to business should be strategic.

- In business, **choosing easy-to-eat foods is more important than selecting messy, sloppy, or gooey personal favorites.**
- In business, **how you communicate with servers says a lot about you.** How you interpret a menu or use utensils can reveal your level of social savvy and also show your communication style, leadership ability, and how much you pay attention to detail.

BUSINESS DINING FROM A TO Z

American Dining Style

Dining styles have names. There's American style, continental style (sometimes referred to as European style), and the "no style." I'm sure you've seen people use "no style." It's not pretty.

When dining American style, hold your fork with the same hand you use to write. In fine restaurants where portions are usually small and the texture is soft, you should be able to eat and cut your food with just your fork.

Three Steps of American Style Dining:

- *First, cut your food holding your fork in your left hand (if you're right-handed) and your knife in your right hand. The fork tines should point downward.*
- *Cut a bite-sized piece of food and set the knife down across the top of the plate.*
- *Transfer the fork to the right hand, holding it in your right hand like a pencil, to pierce or scoop the food and eat.*

Never place your utensils back down on the table or scrape your knife over your fork in midair to remove built up food. Don't draw food off your fork through clenched teeth or allow your tongue to meet your fork before the fork is in your mouth. Leave unused silverware on the table.

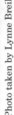

Cutting American Style   *Eating American Style*

Eating **artichokes**: The California Artichoke Advisory Board claims it takes only one try to turn a new artichoke eater into an expert! First, pull off outer petals one at a time. Dip the base of the petal into sauce or melted butter; pull through teeth to remove the soft pulp. Discard the remaining petal and continue until all petals have been removed. Spoon out the fuzzy center at the base; discard. The bottom, or heart, is entirely edible. Cut it into small pieces and dip it into the sauce.

Bread and Butter

How you eat bread can be a moment of truth. Are you going to make a mess or show your mastery?

Bread is usually brought to the table before the first course. Your bread and butter plate is on your left. Ask the server to bring small plates for bread if there are no bread plates, or just use the side of your dinner plate. Butter will be passed separately unless it's preset on your bread plate with a single roll. Take a little more butter than you think you'll need if it's passed separately so you don't have to bother someone on the other side of the table later.

Don't saw your roll in half with a knife. Let your fingers do the breaking unless you are served pre-buttered toast. Tear off a bite-sized piece, butter it, and then eat it. This is done one piece at a time instead of buttering entire slices of bread and slapping the halves together sandwich style.

BEST IN CLASS

Eating **baked French onion soup**: Very tricky. I suggest you don't order it. If you have no choice, remember to use just your spoon. The safest thing to do is move your cheese aside in the bowl and consume only broth. If you're feeling confident, eat the cheese by twirling it around your spoon and pressing it against the side of your soup bowl to "cut" it. Leave the cheese baked on the outside of the crock alone unless you're at home. Allow soup to cool on its own. Never blow on your soup or put ice from your water glass in to cool it.

Continental Dining Style

Another name for continental style is European style, for the very reason the name suggests. It's the style used in most European countries.

Three Steps of Continental Style Dining:

- *Place the fork in your left hand and the knife in your right hand with the handles resting inside your palms and not visible. The fork tines should point downward.*
- *Cut a piece of food using your thumb and index finger to maneuver your fork. Place your index finger across the top of your knife to control your grasp when cutting.*
- *Bring food to your mouth on the tines-down facing fork.*

You don't have to put the knife down and switch your fork to your right hand every time you use it. With this style, you can use your knife in more situations, like easing a stubborn food item onto the fork.

Cutting Continental Style

Eating Continental Style

Eating **crackers**: We just mentioned soup. Add crackers to soup whole, one at a time. It's okay to add oyster crackers a couple at a time. Don't crush a full pack of crackers and then add them to your soup all at once; you'll end up with soup that looks like lumpy oatmeal. Place remaining crackers on your bread plate or the flat plate underneath your soup cup.

Dining Disasters

There are serious offenses at a business meal when your reputation or impression is at stake. Here are some:

- **Being picky by refusing foods that have been preordered for you**, like at a banquet or reception. This is not an episode of Chopped™, the TV show that challenges chefs to turn ingredients into an extraordinary course in a limited amount of time. If you don't like something you've been served, don't ask the chef to prepare something different and then expect your guests to wait until your "replacement meal" arrives. Issue your request for a different meal well in advance of the service or graciously accept what you've been given, without commentary.
- **Sending food back to the kitchen** is a first cousin of refusing foods. Don't make your dining companions wait while the kitchen prepares your steak well done or brings you your vegetables without the butter.
- **Speed dining.** The business meal isn't a race. Slow down, keep the same eating pace as your guests, and focus on business.
- **Pushing your plate away** or stacking your plates when you're finished; that's the server's job.
- **Talking with your hands when holding silverware.** Get a baton if you want to conduct an orchestra.
- **Tucking your napkin into your waist or around your neck.** This is a meal, not a Medieval feast.
- **Offering to leave the tip if you are the guest.** The meal is your host's treat if you were the one invited and that includes the tip. Let your host figure the tip without having to reveal the amount of the bill to you.
- **Not controlling your nervous habits.** Finger drumming, feet tapping, repositioning your utensils for the eleventh time! Have control over what you do with your hands, fingers, feet, and elbows.

- **Choosing the wrong seat.** If you're the guest, wait for the host's signal or ask where you should sit at a formal dinner. If you're the host, point out a chair for each guest, saying "Please sit here" or "Please have this seat—there's a great view of the courtyard." This is very helpful to guests in unfamiliar territory.
- **Leaving the table multiple times during the meal.** Unless you have to clear your sinuses or you're suddenly overcome with a bout of coughing, take your leave before the first course is served. Then return to the table and stay with your dining companions until the meal is finished.
- **Playing with nonfood items.** Turning your straw or the straw wrapper into a craft project is an example. And yes, I've seen foil butter wrappers made into tiny Origami birds. It's clever, but not at a business meal.
- **Leaning back onto the rear two legs of your chair.** If you want to push away from the table, do it safely. Imagine that you would fall completely backwards onto the floor with your feet sticking straight up in the air. I've seen it happen.
- **Taking pictures of your food.** Photographs of people at the meal? Sure. Photographs of people with food? Maybe. In most cases, taking a picture of just your food is a no-no for the business meal unless your boss is the chef. And never make a server wait to serve entrees or clear plates while you take a picture or pass your phone around the table.

> Eating **Dungeness crab**: Crabs are one of the most difficult yet worthwhile foods to consume. As a part-time resident of Maryland's Eastern Shore, I consider myself a crab picking expert. First, break off a leg or claw by pulling it away from the other legs. Crack a section of the leg with your shell cracker and use your hand to open it enough to pull the meat out with your seafood fork. Next, peel back the "tab" at the bottom of the body and pull the whole shell off from the rear. Break the crab down the middle by bending outward from the bottom. Remove the gills on the top of each half. Now take one of the halves and with a knife or your hands cut it in half. If you're using your hands, press down to break the chambers and then pull apart. The lump meat should now be exposed. Use your fingers to pull the meat out and enjoy! (Use your knife to get the meat out of the smaller chambers.)

Entertaining Guests

As an intern or as a first-time professional, there will be opportunities for you to take someone to lunch or even meet for coffee in the morning or afternoon. The most popular meal for business is lunch, but meeting for breakfast or coffee is another option. Breakfasts typically last an hour. Business lunches can be brief or can last into the afternoon. Be considerate of your guest's timeline if they are *crazy* busy (who isn't?). Not everyone has time for a two-hour lunch or coffee. Verbalize the time you expect your meal meeting to end: "Let's meet for lunch for an hour so you can be back in your office by 1:00." Keep an eye on the time, but don't let your guests see you checking your watch.

Here are some rules for entertaining coworkers, potential employers, industry professionals, or internship coordinators when setting up the business meal:

- **Let your guests choose**. When you give your guests a choice of restaurants, you also give them a chance to select a restaurant that accommodates their dietary preferences if they have any. Suggest two or three restaurants you know, preferably those where the staff knows you. Being confident of the quality of the food and service leaves you free to focus on business. If they can't decide, then go ahead and make the decision for them.
- **Make a reservation** if you have a group of four or more; let the staff know you will be dining with clients. Trust me, you'll get better service. Confirm the meal appointment with your clients the day before in an email, a text message, or a voicemail with the restaurant address or location.
- **Arrive early and select a table** that is conducive for business discussion; away from noise, service prep areas, air-conditioning vents, restrooms, or entrances. This is a good time to give your credit card to the maître'd or host/hostess to avoid any awkwardness when the bill arrives if you'll be paying.
- **Take charge of the seating.** Hint: Your guest(s) get the best seats. Make sure people from your organization or department are not all seated together at one end of the table (people tend to sit with people they already know). Mix them in with your guests to allow for the real purpose of the business meal to happen— building relationships with others you don't get a chance to see every day.

Face-to-face time with any business person is a luxury. When we coach professionals in organizations who are having difficulty gaining cooperation or access to someone, we suggest inviting that someone to lunch or coffee. The invitation might surprise them, but if their invitation is accepted, they're a lot closer to building a healthy dialogue with that person than deciphering their emails, dodging their phone calls, or communicating through colleagues.

> Eating **escargot**: When escargot is served as an appetizer in garlic butter, the shell is held in a napkin-covered hand or in a gripper with a scissor-like tong. The snail fork is held in the other hand and used to extract the meat with a pulling motion. Dip the escargot into butter sauce, if provided.

Finished Position

You're finished with your food. How do you communicate that to your server? As mentioned in **Dining Disasters**, do not stack or push away your used plates. (We've even seen a guy place them on the next table!)

Leave your plates in front of you; place the fork next to the knife in a diagonal direction on top of the plate with handles to the right, and the fork tines downward. Turn your knife blade inward. This same position can signal to servers that you're finished with an appetizer or first course.

Finished Position

Don't leave utensils in a non-flat dish (soup cup or bowl, coffee cup, stemmed glass) when your server or bus person comes to clear the table. For example, place a teaspoon on the coffee cup saucer or a dessert spoon on the flat plate under your bowl or stemmed glass.

Note: Used utensils should never touch the surface of the table during or after your meal. *(See **Resting Position**.)*

> Eating **frog legs**: This tender white flesh is like chicken in taste. Eat frog legs with your hands as you would have fried chicken legs in a casual setting. If you're eating them in a fancy restaurant or at a formal affair, separate the joint of a large frog leg with a knife and fork. Hold the leg piece with one hand to eat it.

Giving Thanks

Saying grace before the meal depends on the occasion, the individuals, or the organization. Prayer or reflection can be offered tastefully in many business situations to show respect for diverse religious practices.

Grace and religious rituals might be best observed in the privacy of your home or when you're with a small group of clients or business associates whom you know well. In this case, you can prompt the prayer by saying, "Let's take a moment to give thanks." With new associates or clients whom you've just met, wait until the meals arrive, and everyone has their entrée and then say, "Please, everyone enjoy."

Do your homework regarding the culture or religious practices of the people you're with, especially if it has to do with types of food or consumption of alcohol. (For example, if you're observing Lent, you might offer or order fish or a nonmeat alternative out of respect for your Catholic dining companions.)

When a clergy member is with your group, consider asking him or her to offer "thanks" before the meal. It's a nice gesture and shows respect and acknowledgment. Don't worry about diversity; the clergy person will know what to say and do.

> Eating **grapes**: There are two ways to eat seeded grapes. Break off a branch holding a few grapes if eating a bunch. One way is to lay a grape on its side, pierce the center with the point of a knife and lift and remove the seeds. Another is to put a grape in your mouth, deposit the seeds into your thumb and first two fingers, and place the seeds on your plate.

Handling the Check

Whoever did the inviting does the paying when it comes to business dining. Even if you're the intern and invited the internship coordinator to lunch or coffee, expect to pay the check. If it's a job interview and you've been invited to lunch, your host will take care of the check and the gratuity.

In a served setting as you are seated, mention to the host/hostess that the check will go to you (or someone else in your organization) to avoid the embarrassment or confusion at the end of the meal.

Another option is to say to the server that "my guests" would like to hear the specials, or "my guests" would like to order, etc. at the beginning of service. If you keep saying "my guests," the server should realize you are the host and bring the check to you at the end of the meal. This works most of the time.

Have your credit card ready when the bill comes if you're entertaining clients. Accept the check (usually given in a case or folder), open it to give a quick glance at the bill to make sure it's yours (this is not the time to do a critical survey), and place your credit card inside.

When you're with a group of people at your peer level, offer to pay for your own meal. If you're with supervisors who outrank you, the meal is probably on them, as mentioned. (But be polite about this—bring your wallet with you and don't assume you will always be on the receiving end.) If you are, don't forget to say "thank you."

Let's say you and a group of other coworkers or interns decide to meet for lunch or after work for drinks. Splitting the bill is the norm when professionals socialize with coworkers outside of work. Offer to pay more if you ordered a more expensive item. Calculate quickly and add your share. (This goes for drinks, too.) If others' shares are more than yours and they don't offer to contribute more, either speak up politely or let it go. You could say, "Your share is actually more than half. Why don't you take care of the tip?"

Eating *hors d'oeuvres*: Table manners dictate that hors d'oeuvres are eaten with fingers or a fork, depending on the "where" and "when." Hors d'oeuvres served with cocktails are eaten with fingers. If hors d'oeuvres are passed on trays by the service staff, put the item on a napkin first rather than popping the tasty tidbit into your mouth right from the tray. Hors d'oeuvres served at the table as a first course are eaten with a fork.

Ice Chewing (and Other Annoying Intricacies)

Ice is not an edible part of your meal, so don't chomp on it. This is as bad as talking with your mouth full of food, and it's annoying to others.

Food seems to bring out the worst in people. Whatever you do with your food, the community food (condiments already set on the table), or tableware, be aware of your actions because they can speak volumes about you.

Here, in no order (because they're all annoying) are **some don'ts for consuming food:**

- **Don't repeatedly brush bread crumbs** off the table (that's your server's job) or make them into neat little piles.
- **Don't continuously dab your mouth** with your napkin. If you have to do this, you've probably made a bad decision about what to order or you do not know how to maneuver your utensils properly.
- **Don't cut all of your food at once**. Cut ahead only two to three pieces. You're not in elementary school.
- **Don't overload your fork** and shove huge amounts into your mouth at one time.
- **Don't add more food if your mouth is already full.**
- **Don't gnaw meat off a chop or chicken bone.**
- **Don't talk with food in your mouth.** Your impending comment can wait. Swallow before speaking!
- **Don't use your knife to pick up or transfer food to the mouth.** Twelfth-century dining rules—if there were any—are out.
- **Don't use your fingers when you should be using utensils.** Typical finger foods (French fries, pickles, garnishes) are eaten with utensils when served alongside a meat or entrée that re-

quires utensils. Use your fingers when the entrée is a finger food (sandwich, pizza).

- **Don't blow on hot soup or a drink to cool it.** Stir it quietly and/or wait until it reaches a comfortable temperature.
- **Don't dunk food into a drink.** Yes, it tastes good. No, it doesn't look good.
- **Don't gulp at drinks.** It looks gluttonous.
- **Don't mix primping with food.** Apply lipstick, powder, mascara, or other makeup in the restroom.
- **Don't pick your teeth with a toothpick.** If toothpicks are made available, they're usually next to the after-dinner mints at a location where you leave the restaurant. There's a good reason for this.
- **Don't put the entire bowl of the soup spoon into your mouth.** Sip from the side.
- **Don't butter vegetables.** It's like primping, but with food. Salt and pepper are fine but taste first. (Exception: a baked potation you ordered plain, with butter on the side.)
- **Don't put things passed to you on a tray directly into your mouth.** Place them on your plate or on napkin first. *[See Eating hors d'oeuvres.]*
- **Don't cut spaghetti.** Pick up a few strands and twirl them with your fork against the side of your plate or bowl. No spoons, please!

Eating *ice cream*: Ice cream served in a bowl is eaten with a spoon. Eat berries served atop the ice cream with a fork if one is available. Ice cream served on a plate with a slice of cake or pie is eaten with a fork and spoon; use the fork to hold the cake or pie portion and the spoon to cut and lift the bite to the mouth.

Just Say "No" (Texting and Tweeting During the Business Meal)

Ask almost anyone and they'll tell you that texting, tweeting, and taking calls during any meal, business or social, is rude. And then they do it.

However, there's a digital divide among age groups. A recent survey from the Center for Digital Future at USC's Annenberg School for Communication and Journalism found that 50 percent of twenty-somethings think it's appropriate to text during a meal (only 15 percent of those age thirty and older think the same). If you're at lunch with fifty-year-olds, you should probably put your phone away.

If you *must* use your phone at the table, beforehand verbalize <u>aloud</u> that you're setting a reminder or making a note relevant to the conversation. Don't bury your head in your phone without giving your dining companions fair warning.

The same goes for texting. Verbalize your intent first, or just tell yourself "no" when it comes to texting during a business meal. Don't be tempted to glance at your phone during the meal, especially if it's a job interview. Put your phone away. Being interested in your three-dimensional company is ultimately the best expression of politeness.

Eating *jumbo shrimp*: Shrimp served as hors d'oeuvres are eaten with the fingers. Hold shrimp by the tail and dip it into the cocktail sauce if you prefer; just remember not to "double dip."

Keeping Pace

Are you a fast eater or a slow eater? Ask others who know you and they'll tell you. In the meantime, remember to:

- **Keep the same eating pace as others at your table.**
- **Place your utensils in "finished position" if you're a slow eater and everyone else appears to be finished.**
- **Keep your utensils in "rest position" until everyone appears to be finished** with their meal, even if you finish ahead of them. Don't let the server clear your plate if others are still eating.

Fast eaters beware; if you're clicking and clanging in your soup cup to get the last drop or scraping your plate with a piece of bread to sop up the last drop of sauce, you're finished. When you leave a bite or two of food on your plate, it shows others you're satisfied and not completely focused on food.

Pacing also has to do with courses. If your guests order an appetizer, do the same. If they skip dessert and opt for coffee, skip dessert and order a beverage to enjoy at the same time they have theirs. The business meal is like a dance. Always stay "in step" with your dining companions.

> Eating **kabobs**: Shish kabobs are pieces of meat, seafood, or a combination of both with vegetables cooked on a skewer. Proper etiquette is to use a fork to remove the food from the skewers before eating, starting at the bottom and removing one piece of food at a time. Never eat a kabob by pulling the food off the skewer with your mouth. When the skewer is empty, place it on the side of the plate, not on the table.

Like It or Lump It

You're not going to score points with others by being picky. Especially on a job interview; sending food back to the kitchen or asking for things prepared in a special way for you only shows others that you're hard to please and worse yet, inflexible in a business environment.

Many restaurants today cater to people who are vegetarian, vegan, follow religious guidelines, or have food allergies. I can't believe how many professionals let "pickiness" outweigh the opportunity to create a good impression at a business meal.

We once worked with a young salesperson who frequently took clients to lunch but brought her own food into the restaurant. (She found restaurant food unsuitable.) Her guests thought it was strange and didn't know why they'd been invited to lunch in the first place. She later lost her position with the company. The CEO told me her food aversions were one of the reasons she was dismissed.

Here's how to handle dietary restrictions (of yours and others):

- **Go online and check the restaurant's menu.** Decide ahead of time what you can eat. Call the restaurant if you're not able to eat certain foods for health or religious reasons and find out the ingredients in an item you're interested in ordering.
- **Allow the server to serve you preordered courses or food at a banquet**, even if you don't like or want them. Place your utensils on the plate or in the bowl. Make it look like you're going to eat even if you're not. (Munch on your roll, or sip your iced tea.) It's a lot better than sitting there like a tree while everyone else eats.
- **Order an entrée-sized house salad or a pasta dish.** Many are served with vegetarian sauces.

- **Select a restaurant that appeals to many tastes** and preferences when you're entertaining clients. You may love sushi but be
  considerate and check with your guests first.

Besides showing people how difficult you are to please, being "picky"
or sending food back poses a problem for others dining with you. They
don't know if they should go ahead and eat or wait for your replacement. Just eat what you can and focus on the company. There's always
a Subway™ on the way home.

Handle dietary restrictions diplomatically and gracefully. It will make
a difference and put you (and your dining companions) at ease. Alternatively, if you're given an opportunity to preorder a special meal before a business dining event—usually when you RSVP—by all means
do so. It's not fair to ask the kitchen to prepare a special meal for you
"on the spot" because you forgot to make the request ahead of time.

> Eating *lobster*: When lobsters are served whole, in the shell, you can use your fingers. You should
> have a small fork, a knife, and a nutcracker. Hold the lobster over your plate with one hand. To prevent
> the juice from squirting out from the shell, twist the large claws off slowly and open them with a
> nutcracker. Extract the meat and eat with the small lobster fork. Split the tail and use the fork to lift
> the meat onto your plate. Cut the meat with a knife and dip pieces into sauce with your fork. Rinse
> your fingers in a finger bowl, if one is provided. Discard shells into a bowl, not on the table.

Mastering the Menu

Be familiar with menu terminology. It shows others your level of so-
phistication and can help guide your guests rather than ask the server
a lot of potentially stupid questions.

Speak the language of the cuisine when you order (e.g., French, Italian,
Mexican) if you're fluent. If you're not, don't try to show off for your guests.

Point to an item on the menu if you don't know how to pronounce it.
Say "I'll let the chef decide" if you don't know the answer to the server's
question, "How would you like it cooked?"

Here is a list of foods and preparation techniques to learn:

- **A la carte**: means that each dish is listed separately and individually priced.

- **Aperitif**: an alcoholic drink intended to stimulate the appetite.
- **Bouillon**: a broth of celery, onions, and carrots with herbs, vegetables, and chicken or beef bones.
- **Bruschetta**: Italian toasted bread rubbed with garlic and topped with chopped tomatoes.
- **Canapé**: a small piece of bread or pastry with a savory topping often served as an appetizer.
- **Carpaccio**: thinly sliced raw beef dressed with a mustard sauce. Carpaccio can refer to anything sliced very thinly, like fish or seafood.
- **Ceviche**: a dish of raw fish or seafood marinated in a citrus juice.
- **Chateaubriand**: a think cut from the tenderloin, usually served for two people.
- **Confit**: meat that has been slowly cooked in its own fat (most commonly duck).
- **Consommé**: a clear soup made with richly flavored stock or bouillon.
- **Coulis**: a thick, smooth sauce of pureed fruit or vegetables.
- **Crudités**: raw vegetables, served with a dip usually as an appetizer.
- **Digestif**: an alcoholic drink served after a meal to aid with digestion. Common examples include brandy, cognac, Limoncello™, whisky, and grappa.
- **Du jour**: "as prepared on the particular day" or "of the kind being served today"; this could refer to soup, appetizer, entrée, or dessert dishes.
- **En Brochette**: meat or meat and vegetables (the entrée) served on a skewer.
- **Filet mignon**: a cut of beef taken from the smaller end of the tenderloin.
- **Flambé**: a way of cooking where alcohol such as brandy or cognac is added to a hot pan and ignited to create a burst of flames.
- **Fois gras**: the specially fattened liver of a goose or duck.
- **Ganache**: a sauce made from chocolate and cream.
- **Julienne**: a French term for a method of cutting vegetables into thin strips/matchsticks.
- **Jus** (au jus): a roasted meat served in its own juices.
- **Maitre'd**: a front of the house person; the manager of the service staff.
- **Osso bucco**: An Italian specialty that includes a veal shank, braised with vegetables. Literally translated, osso bucco means

"bone with a hole." When cooked, the marrow in the center of the veal shank melts into the sauce leaving a hole in the middle.

- **Parfait**: a creamy frozen pudding (French) or sundae (American) with layers of ice cream, syrup, cream or liqueur, and fruit.
- **Pate**: a mixture of cooked, ground meat and fat, minced into a spreadable paste. Common additions include vegetables, herbs, spices, and either wine or brandy.
- **Petit fours**: small cakes and biscuits served with coffee.
- **Shank**: a cut of meat from the leg of a calf, sheep, or lamb.
- **Sommelier**: the person responsible for the selection and serving of the wines.
- **Sweetbreads**: the thymus gland (from the throat) or pancreas gland (from the heart or stomach) of calves or lambs.
- **Tartare**: a dish made from finely chopped raw meat or fish, such as steak, venison, tuna, or salmon typically seasoned and served in small cakes.
- **Tempura**: the Japanese name for vegetables or fish deep fried in a light batter.
- **Terrine**: an earthenware dish with a lid in which food is cooked. When on a menu, this refers to what has actually been cooked inside.
- **Welsh rarebit**: a dish of cheese melted with a little ale and served on toast.
- **Yorkshire pudding**: a dish made from batter baked in fat, usually served as an accompaniment to prime rib or roast beef.
- **Zabaglione**: a custard-like dessert made with egg yolks, sugar, and Marsala wine.

Eating *mussels*: When eating mussels served in their shells in broth, remove a mussel from its shell with a cocktail fork, dip into the sauce, and eat it in one bite. For anywhere but a formal dinner, its fine to pick up the shell and a little of the juice, then suck the mussel and juice directly off the shell. The remaining broth can be eaten with a spoon or sopped up with pieces of bread speared on your fork. Yummy!

Napkin Etiquette

The napkin has three places during the meal:

- *On your lap, folded once, with the fold toward you. Don't tuck it into your waistband or into your collar.*

- *On your chair, if you must leave the table during the meal. Place it either on the seat or over the back of your chair.*
- *On the table, to your right, with the soiled (grease or lipstick stains) side downward when you're ready to leave the table at the end of the meal.*

Napkin placement can vary, depending on the formality of the meal. A napkin placed inside a wine goblet usually means the maître'd or your server will place it on your lap. Otherwise, put the napkin on your lap when everyone is seated.

Don't use your napkin repeatedly during a meal or as a hiding place for seeds, pits, or chewing gum (get rid of chewing gum *before* you arrive at the table). Worst of all, don't use your napkin as a handkerchief to clear your sinuses!

Eating **nuts**: Nuts, if dry, are eaten with fingers. When nuts are placed in a common bowl, use a spoon rather than your fingers to place the amount you want to consume on a plate or napkin.

Ordering

Close your menu. It's the universal signal to let your server know you're ready to order. You can also make eye contact and give a nod or say, "We're ready to order now."

Ask your host for one or two recommendations if you're a little nervous and have no idea what to order. You're always safe with staying in the middle price range and ordering lightly. Allow your guests to order first if you're the host. By offering suggestions as they peruse the menu you are indicating a price range. Order the same number of courses as your guests to facilitate the flow of the meal. Remember: **the business meal is not your last supper**.

If servers announce daily "specials" or "chef's selections" not printed on the menu, this does not mean they are specially priced. It's not in your place to ask the price if you're someone's guest; just beware that these recommended specials may be at a *higher* price than what's on the menu.

Don't order the most expensive thing if you're on a job interview meal, no matter how starved you are! This goes for your spouse or partner who may also be invited to a business event that involves ordering from the menu. Again, ask your host for a recommendation. With his or her recommendation, you can gauge a price point to select your entrée. If the host recommends and orders the filet mignon or lobster, then it's okay for you to do the same.

Stick with familiar foods. A business meal shouldn't be the place to order an artichoke for the first time, or a steak prepared "Pittsburgh" (a steak that is charred on the outside and very rare on the inside). The exception to this would be if you're traveling globally and are the guest of international business clients or colleagues. *[See **Understanding Global Differences** in this chapter.]*

Eating raw **oysters**: Take your tiny fork and move the oyster around in its liquid-filled half shell to make sure it's detached. Then put your fork down, pick up the shell, and slurp from the wide end—it's more aerodynamic (smooth) that way. Chew once or twice before you swallow it. If you're at a more formal occasion, spear the oyster with your fork, dip it into the sauce, and eat it in one bite. Then, place each oyster shell upside-down when finished consuming the contents.

Posture, Portfolios, and Purses

Posture counts at a business meal, too. This is not the time to sit back, relax, and let your guard down. Plus, good posture also affects digestion. There is plenty of related data that proves this.

Posture:

- **Don't place your elbows on the table when you lift your fork to your mouth**. Elbows can rest on the table between courses.
- **Don't get up from your seat to reach for something at the table**. Ask for it to be passed.
- **Don't fidget or slouch**. Sit upright and look alert and interested.
- **Keep your hands away from your face** during the meal. If you need to fix your hair, blow your nose, or pick your teeth, do it away from the table.
- **Don't throw your necktie over your shoulder** or worse yet, don't tuck it into your shirt to protect it from being soiled.

- **Don't tuck your napkin into your collar or waist.** Keep it on your lap until you leave the table.
- **Keep enough distance between you and your plate so you can maintain eye contact with someone across the table.** (Exception: when eating soup or spaghetti which require you to bring your head closer to your plate.)

Portfolios and purses:

- **Place purses or portfolios under your chair if they are large** or on your lap if they are small.
- **Never put a purse or portfolio between chairs** where servers need access to serve you.
- **Choose a booth or banquette** if you need access to your purse or portfolio during a business meal. It's a lot easier than reaching under your chair.
- **Never hang anything over the back of your chair.** It's an inconvenience to the servers, especially in a banquet venue where tables are placed close together.
- **Check your coat** before you go to the table. Coats present a problem to servers who need to maneuver between chairs to service the table.

> Eating **poached pears**: Eat poached pears with a spoon and a fork. Use the fork to hold the pear while using the spoon to cut the fruit. If only a spoon is provided, use your hand to rotate the dish and spoon out the sauce or syrup. Leave the core in the dish.

Questions Frequently Asked

The questions we get when we do our "hands on" business dining etiquette programs help us to be prepared with answers in the future. Here are some of those questions (names withheld of course!), along with answers:

- **Is it okay to cut lettuce?** Yes. Use your knife even if you must save it for your entrée. (Hint: when you're finished with your salad, move your knife to the bread plate where it will stay until your main course.)
- **What is a cocktail fork and what do you do with it?** A cocktail fork (usually about half the size of a regular fork, with three

prongs) can be used with an appetizer of raw or cooked oysters, clams, or mussels. It can also be used with a shrimp cocktail in tandem with your fingers.

- **How do you politely get your server's attention?** Never snap your fingers. Use your server's name if you know it. If you don't, use "Sir" or "Ma'am." Eye contact, with an "Excuse me…" also works well when the server passes by your table.

- **Is it ever okay to put your elbows on the table?** Actually, yes. Elbows can be placed on the table between courses, when you don't have food in front of you.

- **Where should I put my used tea bag?** Put used tea bags on the rim of your coffee cup saucer or on your bread plate.

- **How do I take medication at the table?** Use the restroom or take your medication before or after you are with colleagues or guests at a business meal. Dumping your daily supply of pills onto the table at a breakfast meeting could indicate you have medical issues, even if they're only vitamins.

- **Is it ever acceptable to send your meal back?** It is sometimes acceptable to send your meal back, but it should be done with rare exception when you're at the business meal. When a meal is sent back, others at the table don't know if they should wait for your replacement or continue eating. The focus of the meal should be on your guests, not your food. One thing to keep in mind, if you're the host and there appears to be a problem with others' food then take charge. Say something like, "It's obvious that there's a problem with this food. I'm going to request that the server return your meal(s) back to the kitchen."

- **What do you do if someone has already used your water glass?** Request a replacement when convenient for your server, or order a beverage (sparking water, club soda, or something you could have with your meal). Don't make a big deal out of it.

- **What do you do if your napkin falls on the floor?** You can retrieve or leave it. I usually pick mine up. Request another from your server, explaining that yours had fallen onto the floor.

- **Should you eat everything on your plate?** You should leave a bite or two of food on your plate indicating that you're satisfied. It is a visual sign that you have focused on others, not your food, at a business meal.

- **Is it ever appropriate to ask for a doggie bag at a business meal?** No, not at the business meal. Request a doggie bag when you're out with friends or family and then only when half or more of your meal remains uneaten.

- **What is the best way to handle a spill?** If you spill something on yourself, take care of it at the table or excuse yourself and go to the restroom. If you spill something on somebody else, don't dab at it. Instead, apologize sincerely and offer to cover the expense of dry cleaning. Give the person your business card or contact information. If refused, ask the person again at the end of the meal.

- **How many times should I thank the server during the meal?** It's appropriate to acknowledge servers when you're served the first course. You don't have to thank them each time they come to your table. Servers deserve to know if they've given good service. Especially if you're the host, tell them so when you finish your meal.

- **When is it okay to leave the table during the business meal?** It depends on whether you're the host or the guest. If you're the host, try to remain at the table for the entire meal (use the restroom before you take your seat). Otherwise, leave the table between courses and arrive back at the table before the next course is served. Don't make dining companions (or servers) feel they must wait for your return to serve the next course or begin eating.

- **What is the best way to squeeze a lemon wedge?** Spear the lemon wedge with your fork and hold the lemon wedge or lemon half (over the food or beverage) and twist the prongs of your fork.

- **How do I remove pits or seeds?** Don't spit pits or seeds into your napkin. Bring your fork or spoon to your mouth and remove them, placing them on the side of your plate. Fish bones can be removed with your fingers.

Eating **quesadillas**: In Mexico, you eat quesadillas with your hands. If a quesadilla is served with salsa, sour cream, or other sauces, and is very hot—you can use your knife and fork to cut and eat it. Depending on the filling, folded quesadillas are easier to pick up and eat with your fingers.

Resting Position

Rest position is a way for you to silently signal to your server that you are "between bites." It also helps servers know whether to approach your table to clear plates or prepare for the next course.

Continental Style Rest Position:

Between bites, place your knife and fork crisscrossed on your plate, in a position to easily retrieve them and continue eating. The tines of your fork should be downward-facing, as this is the position of your fork when you bring it to your mouth.

American Style Rest Position:

Between bites, place your knife across the top of your plate (blade inward) and your fork diagonally as shown in the diagram. Do not leave half-eaten food on the fork when you put it down.

Never sit between bites with your knife and fork held like this:

BEST IN CLASS

> Eating **rice** with chopsticks: Don't be a wimp and use your fork. If 40 percent of the world's population can do this, so can you! Chinese etiquette says that you may lift the bowl of rice close to your mouth. Scoop the rice up; don't shovel the rice into your mouth. The rice will be sticky, so that makes it a lot easier to eat using your chopsticks—almost like a spoon.

Small Talk

The purpose of a business meal is business, as mentioned numerous times in this chapter. Start your meal with casual conversation if you don't know your business guests or clients well. If you have an established business relationship, you can eliminate some of the chitchat when time is an issue.

Safe small talk topics are *current events, leisure activities, family, pets, sports, entertainment, the arts, or the weather*. Don't get too personal. Some people don't like to discuss their personal lives, so family discussions might be off-topic until you get to know them better. Topics that could pose uncomfortable discussion are the all-time tragic trio of *politics, money, and religion*. Unless you really know your dining companions, stay away from those.

Don't wait too long to discuss business or your clients might start to wonder why they were invited. On the other hand, if you begin too early in the meal, your guests might suspect that you are more interested in their business than you are in them. Engage in small talk up until your first course or entrée arrives, which is a comfortable amount of time before transitioning to business.

> Eating **sushi**: Sushi is eaten with chopsticks or fingers. Dip only the fish side into the accompanying soy sauce so that the sticky rice won't break up. Bring the piece of sushi to your mouth and eat it in one bite.

Tipping Guidelines

Be savvy about tipping. Learn how to add the tip onto your check quickly and accurately. Always give your check a cursory glance to make sure that the tip has not already been added for you. In some restaurants, the tip will be added for parties of six people or more.

Currently, some restaurants are piloting a no-tipping process because of the inequity in compensation for servers and kitchen staff. Alternatively, some restaurants include a separate line item for you to tip kitchen staff. Either way, be familiar with the restaurant tipping policies or discretely ask a manager before you pay your bill.

HERE ARE SOME TIPPING PRINCIPLES:

Servers (Waiter/Waitress)	15%–20% OF THE PRETAX AMOUNT
Sommelier (Wine steward)	10%–20% OF THE COST OF THE WINE DEPENDING ON THE HELPFULNESS IN SELECTING THE WINE
Bartender	15% AT THE BAR; 20% IF SERVED AT A TABLE IN THE BAR/ LOUNGE AREA
Coat Check	$1–$2 PER COAT

Calculating 20% is easy. If the total bill was $50, tip $10. You can take off a dollar or two to avoid tipping on the tax or if you want to give less than 20 percent. Use a credit card to add the tip easily and keep track of your expenses. The rules to tipping have international interpretations, so follow the guidelines we suggest in the next section, Understanding Global Differences.

My Mother enjoyed a part-time job as a coat check attendant at a local restaurant when she was in her retirement years. It was her "window to the world" on Friday and Saturday nights. She gave special attention to briefcases, expensive coats, umbrellas, or hats. If you encounter "scrupulous" coat check attendants and you have the urge to tip more than the norm, know that—like my Mother—it will thrill them.

> Eating **cherry tomatoes**: These are the tomatoes that compare in size to a golf ball and are placed atop a salad, whole. They can become a gushy projectile if you pop them into your mouth whole! First, pierce the tomato with the tines of your fork to release the pressure. Then use your knife to cut it in half.

Understanding Global Differences

Knowing the nuances of global differences in business dining will help you blend in and demonstrate an understanding and respect for a different culture. You will impress your colleagues if, early in your career, you have a sense for what is appropriate behavior in an international business environment.

Whether you're at home in the United States with international guests or visiting an international location and hosting a meal, keep these general guidelines in mind:

- **Invitations are to be accepted.** You'd better have a good excuse if you're going to refuse an invitation for a business meal from an international client or colleague. *Always* try to accept an invitation for any business-social occasion. It's a compliment to be invited, so treat it as such.
- **Seating is strategic.** Most seating arrangements are planned by your international host. Know who will be seated next to you and across from you. And before you grab a seat and plop down, first ask where you should sit.
- **Pacing is slower.** Americans are always in a rush, so observe the pace of others at your table and maintain the same pacing.
- **Timelines are different.** For example, in Germany, ten minutes early is "on time." In Brazil, thirty minutes late is "on time."
- **More focus is on the food and the people** than on the topic of business. If business is to be discussed, let your international guests initiate that discussion.
- **"Hamburger mentalities" need not apply.** Be open-minded about trying new foods and do not criticize a food recommended by your international dining companions if you don't like it. Thank them for the recommendation and acknowledge that the taste is "different" or "unexpected." If you love it, then say so!
- **You can ask for help when interpreting the menu.** It's not rude to inquire if you don't speak the language.
- **Small talk matters.** Appropriate topics vary from culture to culture, so know which ones are taboos for the country or culture. If you're asked, express your opinions without getting confrontational. (Remember, just because it's different doesn't mean it's wrong.)
- **"Please" and "thank you," when spoken in the native tongue, mean a lot.** Learn a few phrases and words to show appreciation and respect for the culture. Start with "please" and "thank you."
- **Servers are people, too.** Just like in the United States, treat servers and staff with respect. All eyes are on you.
- **Learn to use chopsticks** if you're in Asia. Use the continental dining style if you're in Europe. Avoid using your left hand if you're in the Middle East.
- **Tipping norms are different.** Overtipping can be as offensive as no tipping in some countries. There are also countries where a tip of any kind can be offensive. Know tipping rules in advance.

Be a follower rather than a leader when you're the guest in an international venue. Don't expect that U.S. dining norms carry over to other countries because they don't. Chances are there will be someone with you whom you trust and you can observe.

> Eating **udon**: Udons are soft, thick, and chewy Japanese noodles served in a broth. Udon noodles are eaten with chopsticks and the broth is eaten with a spoon.

Vintage Rules and Toasts

Don't let your lack of knowledge force you to give up control of the wine selection. There are many websites and reference books with basic information about wine. Check them out if you know you'll be hosting a meal that includes ordering wine.

I've heard many horror stories about professionals who—in a gesture of courtesy—relinquish control of the wine list to a client or dinner guest. You know the rest of the story. The guest orders a $200 bottle of wine which could never be explained in an expense account.

For starters, white wine is served with fish and poultry and red wine with meat. There are exceptions.

Ordering wine:

- **Ask the wine steward** (sommelier) to tell you and your guests about the house wines and to make a recommendation based on what you have ordered.
- **There are about four to six full-sized (four- to six-ounce) glasses per standard bottle.**
- **Point to the wine on the menu if you're ordering something you can't pronounce.** Just say, "We would like this bottle" instead of embarrassing yourself.

Serving wine:

- **When the bottle is presented to you** (and before it's opened), **acknowledge with a nod** that this is the wine you ordered, checking the label, vintage, and/or date.
- **After it has been opened, check the cork for moistness** and to see that wine stains do not run the full length of the cork, which could indicate leakage. A cork should never be dry and crumbly.

- **When wine is poured for you to taste, taste to determine that the wine is not "flawed."** You're not tasting to determine if you like it. The assumption is that when you ordered the wine, you had enough knowledge to know how it should taste and that your choice would be compatible with the meal.
- **When tasting wine, remember the two "Ss": swirl and smell.** You're swirling the wine to release the aroma. If you like what you smell, you'll like the taste.
- **After you've tasted** and judged the wine acceptable, **give a final nod to the server** who will proceed to pour for your guests. If the server is knowledgeable, then he or she will pour starting with the first female to your right.

Consuming wine:

- **Hold the glass from the stem** rather than the globe or bowl. This prevents your body temperature from warming the wine if it's white, and allows you to enjoy its clarity if it's red.
- **Be sure that each of your guests has had sufficient wine** as the host. Offer to replenish glasses if they're empty. (Guests should never have to refill their own glasses.) Red wine is filled to halfway up the glass; white wine is filled to three-fourths of the glass.
- **Say "no thank you" to the server if you don't want more wine.** If you *do* want more wine, don't lift your wine glass for the server to refill; a moving target could be difficult for a server to hit. Leave your glass in place on the table.

Don't make wine tasting a big production or try to show off for your guests. It's really a quick process. A sommelier shared with me that only 10 percent of bottles returned by patrons are actually bad. Unfortunately, people who claim a wine is bad are usually unfamiliar with the wine they ordered and sometimes request a replacement just to impress guests.

Toasting etiquette. The intent of a toast is to acknowledge someone or acknowledge an event or a success. Proper toasting etiquette dictates that the person(s) being toasted do not drink. (Compare it to patting yourself on the back.) The recipient of the toast can remain seated and respond with thanks or stand and offer another toast. The host is always the first person to offer a toast.

© g-stockstudio/Shutterstock.com

Toasts do not mean you must drink alcohol (wine or champagne). It's traditional to have wine, sparkling wine, or champagnes, but sparkling fruit juice, punch, or even soft drinks can be used. Never toast with water—it's actually considered bad luck. If you don't have another beverage, toast with an empty glass. Not participating in a toast is considered rude and sends a negative message.

If you're in a large group, you don't have to clink your glasses when the toast is made. Just raise your glass and take a sip. If you're in a small group, always make eye contact with the person when you clink his or her glass. It's considered inappropriate to applaud after a toast is made; the clinking or the verbal salutation is enough.

> Eating **vermicelli**: Vermicelli is a thin form of rice noodles that resemble spaghetti in length and thickness. Twirl strands of vermicelli or spaghetti with your fork; do not use your knife to cut them. Try to pick up two or three strands with each bite to avoid a bite that becomes too large. For leverage, balance the tips of the tines against the side of the plate and wind the strands around them. Bring the fork to your mouth and use your teeth to bite off long strands rather than slurp them up. The American custom of using a spoon to assist in twirling is just that—an American custom. If you want to eat vermicelli or spaghetti the authentic way, use only your fork.

Where to Find What

Table settings can vary slightly from restaurant to restaurant. If you know the basics (drinks on the right and food [salad and/or bread plate] on the left) you'll be fine.

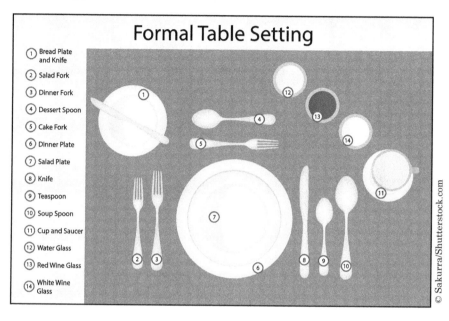

Formal Table Setting

1. Bread Plate and Knife
2. Salad Fork
3. Dinner Fork
4. Dessert Spoon
5. Cake Fork
6. Dinner Plate
7. Salad Plate
8. Knife
9. Teaspoon
10. Soup Spoon
11. Cup and Saucer
12. Water Glass
13. Red Wine Glass
14. White Wine Glass

© Sakurra/Shutterstock.com

All utensils, except in some cases the butter knife and the dessert fork or spoon, will be placed parallel. The cutting edges of the knives are always placed inward. There will be enough room between your utensils for a dinner plate, so don't move your utensils around just because you're left-handed, for example. Never rearrange or move your dinner plate once it has been placed in front of you.

When eating, start with the utensils on the outside of the place setting and work inwards for each course.

Eating **wings**: This little known wing-eating trick for flat chicken wings (the ones with two bones) will help you eat wings without missing any meat. Find the end with a larger amount of bone sticking out. Pull the little piece of cartilage at the end. You can eat this if you want. Locate the little bone (the skinny one) and twist it until it comes loose. Pull it out; it should come out completely clean. Repeat the process with the bigger bone. If any meat comes out, you can just suck it off. This will yield a boneless chicken wing which you can eat and enjoy! Note: Drumsticks are easy. You know how to eat those!

© DGLimages/Shutterstock.com

MiXing Business with Booze

Early in my career as a speaker, I attended a cocktail reception with clients before my program the next day. A group of women all ordered the same cocktail, "Sex on the Beach." They were giggling and telling everyone (including the senior partners and invited guests) about their drinks. The company president politely chuckled but looked terribly uncomfortable.

Bottom line: there's nothing wrong with ordering that drink. ("Sex on the Beach" is made with vodka, peach schnapps, Chambord, and fruit juice.) What's wrong is *when* and *where* it is ordered. For example, you wouldn't order a "Kamikaze" with a Japanese sales agent.

If you're going to be drinking while "on business," have a go-to drink (mentioned below)—that is, something you can order quickly and not make others wait while you make your decision about what to drink. This could be something simple: a glass of the house chardonnay, a vodka and tonic, or even a draft beer.

For occasions, when you mix booze with business, keep these in mind:

- **Always stay in professional mode,** even though you aren't in the office. Your conduct after-hours—positively or negatively—

can impact your career. Happy hour is the "perfect storm" where you can make a good impression, but it could go the other way.

- **Know that it's okay to have a drink.** Many of your biggest opportunities to advance your career will be at events where alcohol is served, so don't think you have to avoid alcohol altogether. You might miss out on valuable face time with colleagues, clients, or potential decision makers if you consistently skip the office happy hour.

- **Participate, even if you choose not to drink.** It's okay to opt out of consuming alcohol for personal, religious, or health reasons. But, you don't have to carry the banner on alcohol avoidance with you to the business meal or event if you're a nondrinker. You should make an effort to allow those around you to feel comfortable having a drink themselves. You can say, "No thanks, I'm not drinking tonight, but please, go ahead." This approach also works in a situation when you definitely do not want to consume alcohol but know it's *never* appropriate—like a job interview meal.

- **Have a "go-to" drink** so others don't have to wait for you to make a selection. Keep it simple; you're not impressing others if they have to wait for you to explain your version of mixology to the bartender.

- **Know your audience and how they will view what you drink.**

- **Follow what others are doing.** This goes for business meals. If they order a drink, *you* can, too. If they don't, *you* don't. (If you're unsure, order something nonalcoholic. You can always grab a drink later.)

- **Limit yourself.** Know that increased physical activity and dehydration (like after a golf game), combined with alcohol can be dangerous. Pace yourself—it's not a race.

- **Stick to your selection.** Choose wine, mixed drinks, or beer.

- **Stay away from pitchers** unless ordering food and at least three people are drinking the same beer.

- **Ask for a glass.** That's the rule when ordering bottled beer. The exception: a sporting event where glassware is unavailable or when you're with family or friends.

- **Never drink on an empty stomach.** Eat before you get there, and again during happy hour. Mixed nuts are your friend.

- **Keep your beverage in your left hand** so you can shake hands with your right hand when you're at a networking or business event.

To avoid getting tipsy:

- **Set a limit for yourself**, usually two drinks. If you don't have a limit, two glasses of wine can easily become three, four, or more. If you've reached your limit, you can still fit in by ordering a club soda with lime. Decide how much you'll drink over a specific time frame and stick to it. And remember, this is not the same limit you'd set for a night out with your friends.
- **Have an arrangement with the server**. When you order a second gin and tonic, you get only the tonic. This is an old trick, but one that has been time-tested.
- **Dilute your drink**. Order your scotch with water or weaken your drink subtly by adding water from your water glass.
- **Order a sidebar**. Along with your chardonnay, order a glass of club soda or tonic water with lime, and alternate your sips: one sip of wine, then one sip of club soda or tonic.
- **Order a drink that is not your favorite**, and nurse that drink throughout the meal. If you'd rather have beer than wine with your meal, order the wine.

I am often asked how many drinks can someone safely and respectably order at a business meal or networking reception. There is no easy answer, but most seasoned professionals we've consulted for this book say that ordering one or two drinks is the norm. Ordering a third drink raises an eyebrow, no matter your level of tolerance.

Don't overindulge in alcoholic beverages at the business meal. As I've mentioned many times, **it's still business.** Having fun is *not* your primary objective. Have a plan to avoid getting intoxicated, or simply don't drink alcohol. Know your limits, no matter who you're with, and how much you feel you need to "take the edge off" during an important occasion. If your guests have overindulged, make arrangements for their transportation home.

> Eating **XO sauce**: This spicy sauce, first created in Hong Kong, is known as the "caviar of the East." It is quickly gracing tables at Asian restaurants across North America. The classy sauce was associated with "XO," the esteemed cognac designation but contains no brandy. It is used to enhance the flavor of stir-fried meat, seafood, tofu, and vegetables and includes a combination of dried shrimp, dried scallops, garlic, and other seasonings. Treat it like a high-powered soy sauce and use it sparingly.

Yours or Mine? (Sharing Community Food)

The rule is simple regarding the passing and sharing of food; offer to someone first before you help yourself.

Community food includes whatever is set in the middle of your table for everyone to share. Salad dressings, butter, bread, sugar, cream for coffee, and other condiments are examples. Salt and pepper, also a community food, are passed together even if the request is only for the salt. If someone asked for a community food to be passed to them, pass it to them first before helping yourself.

There is a process for properly sharing community foods. If you're seated closest to the community food, *you* should initiate the passing by offering it to the person on your left (hold out the bread basket, for example), then help yourself and continue passing to the right. I know, you think the person on your left will continue to pass to the left and you won't have the chance to help yourself. Just politely ask for the item to be passed back to you if it lands in the middle of the table and remember, **this isn't your last supper**.

> Eating **Yorkshire** pudding: Referred to as "the most glorious dinner-sponge ever created," Yorkshire pudding is an English side dish made from batter consisting of eggs, flour, and milk. It is served with beef and gravy and sometimes as a dessert.

Zealous Servers

Polite communication with the wait staff is crucial to making a good impression during a business meal. Interacting rudely with the wait staff can send mixed messages about how you would treat subordinates and others in the workplace. Dave Barry, Pulitzer Prize–winning columnist said, "A person who is nice to you but rude to the waiter is not a nice person."

Here are some tips for dealing with wait staff:

- **Make eye contact with your servers** when they greet you at your table or when they tell you about the menu.
- **Never whistle or snap your fingers** to get their attention. Try to catch their eye and then politely say their name or "Sir" or "Ma'am."
- **Make your requests in a considerate way**, especially if they are very busy. For example, "When you get a chance, could you please give us more bread?"
- **Don't bully them if something goes wrong**. It's not your server's fault if your meal is not properly cooked.
- **Express your concern in a controlled manner** and with a polite tone of voice. Ask to speak to the manager *after* you say goodbye to your clients or guests.
- **Never leave without tipping.** Leave a 10 percent tip if you really had problems with the waiter.
- **Mention to servers that you'd like a slower pace of service**, if they appear to be overdoing it with a little more zeal than necessary. This gives them an indication that you may want some privacy and except for the primary progress of the meal and the courses you ordered, you'd prefer to be left alone with your guests.

Never be rude or patronizing to the wait staff, no matter how inexperienced they are. Servers are people, too. Acknowledge your servers, but don't thank them every time they refill your water glass.

> Eating *ziti*: Wide noodles like ravioli, lasagna, or ziti are cut and eaten with a fork. If pasta is served in a deep bowl, ziti is eaten with a spoon.

A DIGESTIF ON THE BUSINESS MEAL

The business breakfast, lunch, or dinner may not be your comfort zone, but it *will* open new relationships and opportunities for you.

Once you've shared a meal with others, they are more likely to open their communication with you. Use the business meal to dialogue and solve problems as much as you use it to open doors. You'll be surprised to discover how many professionals will welcome a much-needed break in their schedules by going out to breakfast, lunch, or dinner.

Always remember to never let your guard down. The business meal may be in a relaxed atmosphere, but it is still business and your actions speak volumes. **The business meal is not your last supper.** Focus on people and business rather than food. There's always a fast-food restaurant around the corner on your way home.

IS THE LUNCH INTERVIEW A BAD SIGN?

© mavo/Shutterstock.com

Quite the contrary. Many second and third job interviews are scheduled around a business meal; that's <u>not</u> a coincidence. Hiring managers can tell a lot about you and how organized you are and how much you pay attention to detail by the way you conduct yourself at the table. The business meal *isn't* a time to relax and let your guard down.

There are other reasons *why* an employer will choose to conduct an interview over lunch. The hiring manager many not want office staff to know the company is hiring for a particular position, or you may be invited on a lunch because you're the leading candidate and you're being evaluated to see if you can handle yourself gracefully under pressure. The employer wants to see how your "social skills" work for you in a business setting.

Here are some dining tips for the job interview lunch:

- **Arrive early.** Wait outside the dining room in a waiting area. Don't go to a table and order an iced tea and begin munching on the breadsticks.
- **Learn about the restaurant in advance.** Not just to peruse the menu to see what you're up against, but also to find out about the establishment to share something about *you* to the hiring manager you're meeting. An example, *"I found out that this building was once a bank in the 1930s. Actually, I'm a history buff, and the 1930s are particularly interesting to me."*
- **Wear an appropriate interview outfit,** even if the restaurant is more casual than the company office.
- **Turn off your phone.** Put it away so you won't be tempted to glance at it during the interview, even if you decide halfway through the meal that you're no longer interested in the job. Don't check it even if others at the table are looking at their phones.
- **Put your napkin on your lap** as soon as you're seated; put it on the chair if you leave the table and put it on top of the table as you get up to leave when the meal is over.
- **Know your territory.** Liquids on the right, food on the left. (Pssssst...your bread pate is on the left; your water glass is on the right.)
- **Don't order alcohol.** Interviewing is tough enough without adding alcohol to the mix.
- **Don't order messy food.** That can include pasta with sauce, chicken with bones, ribs, finger foods, and big sandwiches. Order something that's easy to cut into bite-sized pieces. Good choices are chopped salads, bite-sized pasta with a light sauce, cooked fish). Take small bites and finish chewing and swallowing before speaking.
- **Don't order the most expensive thing.** This could send the wrong message and besides, the focus is *not* on food during a job interview meal.

- **Be prepared to small talk.** See "Small Talk" under Business Dining from A to Z. Keep the conversation light toward the start of the meal. By now, you should also have done your homework on the company, so you can ask intelligent and relevant questions. Ask questions of the hiring manager, too; for example, *"How did you begin your work with the company?"*
- **Say "please" and "thank you"** to your server and your host. Also, chew with your mouth closed, sit up straight, and never speak with your mouth full of food.
- **Hold utensils correctly.** A meal—especially a job interview meal—is a test to see how well you pay attention to detail and comparatively, how well you'll pay attention to detail in your job. Every little detail counts.
- **Let the prospective employer pick up the tab.** The person who invited you will expect to pay both the bill and the tip.

BUSINESS ETIQUETTE AFTER HOURS

"The goal of war is peace, of business, leisure."
—ARISTOTLE

This isn't the time to cross the boundaries of professionalism. What happens outside the office at after-hours events can be one of the most critical (and ultimately successful) aspects of conducting business.

Here are some ways to enjoy business-after-hours events, while observing professional etiquette:

- **Keep your organization's culture in mind.** Peter Drucker, American management consultant and author, said, *"Culture eats strategy for breakfast!"* Work hard but observe your company's social culture. In other words, find out the unwritten rules about alcohol, for example, and what behavior is acceptable at casual events.
- **Set goals.** Plan your strategy. If you don't usually get a chance to talk with leadership and heads of the department, make certain you spend a couple of minutes with them. Seek out people from

other departments to expand your internal network. Come to the conversation prepared with some simple questions. Good examples are:

- *How is the XYZ project going?*
- *What have been some of your favorite projects?*
- *How long have you been a part of this organization?*
- *What do you like to do when you're not working?*

Stick with simple questions. You can get in-depth later.

- **Be a good listener.** Commit to listening more than talking, especially when you have a chance to talk with organizational leaders. Listen to people in other departments, too. Work is not the only topic to discuss at after-hours events, and the after-hours events are not the time to discuss office gossip. Ask questions about sports, movies, books, vacation, travel, and pets—all are good topics. By connecting with people from other departments on a personal level you might create possible mentors, references, and contacts that can help your career down the line.
- **Be professional but be yourself.** This is not your personal happy hour, it's an extension of your workday and is still considered a business setting. Pay attention to how you're dressed because you're still giving others an opportunity to get an impression of you.

- **Don't hog the food or get drunk.** Always uphold professionalism and be aware of what you are drinking and know your limits. There are some cultures where the vodka is flowing at after-hours events, and other cultures where you're given drink tickets to control the consumption of alcohol. Have a snack before you arrive so you won't be tempted to attack the hors d'oeuvres table. Hold your drink *or* plate in your left hand (not both), keeping your right hand free to offer a friendly and firm handshake. No matter where you are, remember also *not* to drink and drive.

NETWORKING THAT'S NOT WORKING

"...good schmoozers are good listeners, not good talkers."
—GUY KAWASAKI

Social media "friends" and "connections" are great—if you do something with those connections. But remember that any tool that is easy or automated won't establish the connections you really need in business. That's why you must network to maintain those connections or build relationships.

Six thousand executives at three thousand companies in the United States and Europe found that executives with 50 percent more professional contacts above the average had a salary of 3.5 percent or $15,000 higher than their less *sociable* contacts. The conclusion may be simple: Increase your professional contacts and get a higher salary.

Do the math. The average person knows 150 to 200 people reasonably well. The number of social connections we can actively maintain is 150, according to evolutionary psychologist Robin Dunbar. "Dunbar's Number" is a suggested cognitive limit to the number of relationships in which an individual knows who each person is and how each person relates to every other person. If you meet someone at a networking event for the first time, you have access to 150 more people than you knew before meeting him or her. Meet two people and you have access to 300 more people. And so on...

When it comes to networking, some approaches work better than others. There was an actual study that revealed people who networked in the "selfish" way—to pitch their organization and form one-sided professional contacts—described networking as *uncomfortable*, even *sleazy*. Those who network to build a personal connection with others in their industry gave more clean, positive words to describe the networking experience.

No matter how you describe it, networking works. Make it work for you by avoiding these common mistakes that could sabotage your networking efforts:

Networking Mistakes

- **Not having a plan.** Arrive a little early or on time. Check the name tags on the table when you register and target two or three people you want to meet during the event, why you want to meet them, then seek them. You can't do that if you arrive late. There may be an attendee list available online when you register for the event. If so, you can do all this ahead of time, and you'll approach the networking event with more confidence. Always be prepared when you go to a networking event with a pen to jot things down, and your business cards.
- **Wearing your name tag on the wrong side.** Your nametag goes on your **right** shoulder so it's visible to the person facing you. It may feel silly to wear a nametag, but it allows the other person to easily glance at your name for a quick refresher. Wear your nametag high on your shoulder so it's visible and use the other person's name in conversation, too. Some organizations request their employees place nametags on the left, and uniforms are designed to accommodate that. The reason for this is like the rationale for military insignia which is worn on the left side; it's always placed over the heart.
- **Not leaving your friends.** You can arrive with your friends, maybe even *double up* and have a friend serve as your personal PR agent at meetings or networking events. At some point, split up and meet people individually then and come back together and introduce each other to new acquaintances. Don't cling to others you work with and see every day, especially if your purpose is to meet others.

- **Tentative body language.** A **smile** tells others that the coming introduction will be pleasurable. Don't walk into the room like you're about to experience a root canal. Look approachable, **keeping your hands visible**, not tucked into your pockets or behind your back. **Eye contact** matters enormously in face-to-face venues. Make eye contact with the person you're speaking with 60 percent of the time so that it doesn't look like you are staring or darting your eyes about the room. Have a **firm handshake** and look the person in the eye while you're initiating a handshake. Don't infringe on other people's territory by standing too close (three to five feet is a comfortable distance in the American culture). In a noisy room where you need to get closer to talk, people will understand. In this case, make sure your breath is fresh and you're not spitting food while talking.
- **Not approaching others.** Pay attention to the body language of others. If people are standing in "V-shaped" twosomes or threesomes, they're more approachable. In other cases when there's someone in the group you want to meet, rather than barging into a conversation, approach and stand quietly for a second or two. They will notice you. If they *don't* acknowledge you, exit immediately with an "excuse me." Also, look for odd numbered groups of individuals which are also easier to approach because the conversation is usually more casual.
- **Not knowing how to introduce yourself.** Break the ice by taking this three-step approach to *starting* a conversation:
  1. Observe something positive that you have in common with the other person: *"This event is certainly well planned and well attended."*
  2. Disclose something about yourself: *"This is the first time I've been at a Rotary business-after-hours event."*
  3. As a question: *"How about you? Do you attend these events each month?"*

Research from Harvard University confirms what all great conversationalists know: People like to talk about themselves, so encourage conversation by asking questions.

When people ask, *"What do you do?"*, you should be able to tell them in ten seconds by giving an interesting and engaging pitch. Here are two options you can use:

1. I-We-Our Organization [*provides/offers/produces*]
[*produce or service*] **to help/give**
[*your clients*] **to/a/the** [*feature/benefit*].

OR

2. I [*what you do in your job*] **so that**
[*why your job is important/how you help your customers/clients*].

- **Business card bashing.** No matter how proud you are of your
  first official business card, giving a handful of your cards to one
  person could be perceived as asking him or her to "sell" for you.
  That's *your* job, not theirs. On the other hand, there is nothing
  more unprofessional then having to say, *"Oh, I'm sorry I just
  handed out my last card..."* Never leave the house or your office
  without your business cards. Here are some guidelines for business card exchange:
  - Make sure your business card is presentable, not crumpled or
    dirty.
  - Give your business card to someone when they ask for it or
    when you can verbalize the reason you're asking for someone
    else's card: *"Let's exchange cards so I can reach out to you
    about the next networking event."*
  - Use your right hand to offer your card, holding it by the top
    corner, facing the other person.
  - Make a positive comment about the other person's card when
    you receive it. (You like the logo, business name, etc.)
  - Put the other person's card away gently. Don't stuff it in your
    wallet or the back pocket of your handbag. (Enter the infor-
    mation in a database afterwards.)
  - Don't ask for the business card of one individual in front of a
    group of people.
- **Not knowing how to disengage.** Notice if the person you're
  talking to begins to scan the room, looking for someone else to
  talk to. Don't hold the person hostage. That's your cue to say, "It
  was great to meet you" and excuse yourself. If it's you who wants
  to move on (perpetually boring people are everywhere), make a

statement (*"I need to say hello to _____"* or *"I'm sure you need to say hello to some others who are here"*). Then leave the conversation, moving at least one-fourth of the room away so that your moving on appears purposeful.

- **Not being a good listener.** Be interested in others and they will find *you* interesting. Ask open-ended questions, beginning with the journalist's five Ws (Who, What, When, Where, Why, and also How). My favorite is, *"How's business?"*
- **Not following up.** As mentioned earlier, connections are great *if* you do something with them. Just because you have the person's business card, or you met someone at a networking event, he or she is not part of your network unless you connect at another time. Follow up with a hand-written note on your company's stationery, invite your new business friend for coffee, send the person an email or text (if you have a mobile number), invite the person to connect on LinkedIn or to join you for lunch. Make a habit of adding people you meet at networking events to your contacts list.

THE THIRTY-SECOND ELEVATOR PITCH

"Networking is marketing. Marketing yourself, marketing your uniqueness, marketing what you stand for."
—CHRISTINE COMAFORD-LYNCH

An "elevator speech" is a clear, brief (thirty seconds or less) message or "commercial" about you. It communicates who you are, what you're looking for, and how you can benefit a company or organization. This is not the time to be shy or modest about presenting yourself as an interesting and competent person.

Elevator pitches can accomplish many goals, including:

- Introducing yourself (career fairs, conferences, conventions, networking events)
- Facilitating seeking help in a professional setting
- Establishing a business relationship
- Gaining visibility in your industry or organization

- Marketing yourself or your organization
- Expanding your personal/professional network
- Giving you access to individuals who are difficult to reach

Elevator pitches should be practiced and memorized but delivered to sound natural rather than rehearsed.

Your elevator pitch should contain four parts:

1. **Who you are.** Your name, current position, or position you're seeking.

   Hi, I'm Liz Atherton. I'm a senior environmental sciences major looking for a position where I can use my research and analysis skills.

   I'm Brett Bando. I'm a senior studying computer information science, planning to be a computer programmer when I graduate.

   Hi, my name is Justin Lauer. I'm a sophomore at the University of South Carolina majoring in business. I'm particularly interested in the area of finance.

BEST IN CLASS

2. **Your personal strengths and/or distinguishing information.** What problems have you solved? What contributions have you made in related jobs or industries?

(Liz) ...I've been [using my research skills] working with a local watershed council on conservation strategies to support water quality and habitats.

(Brett) ...I've had a couple of internships where I worked on several program applications with a project team.

(Justin) ...This summer I did an internship with the Groundhog Hedge Fund Group and I hope to work in USC's credit union when I return to school this fall.

3. **What you can do for others or how you can help others.** What can you offer? How have you helped others? What would be the advantages of working with/getting to know you? How are you different from other people who do what you do?

(Liz) ...Eventually, I'd like to develop education programs on water conservation awareness.

(Brett) ...I enjoy developing computer applications for simple business solutions.

(Justin) ...I've always been interested in numbers and I know this is what I want to do in my career. I love helping people with their finances and had a blast this year preparing a presentation as part of a team for my business statistics class.

4. **How you can be contacted or how you plan to follow up.** How will you follow up with your listener? When, where, how can they reach you?

(Liz) ...I read that your organization is involved in water quality projects. Can you tell me how someone with my experience would fit into your organization and who I could contact to follow up?

(Brett) ... I'd like to hear more about the types of project teams in your organization. The position you have listed on LinkedIn would be a perfect fit for someone with my skills, and I'm looking for an opportunity with a company of your size and scope.

(Justin) ...Here's my card with my email address. I can also be reached on my mobile phone; that number is also there. Please tell me, who can I follow up with from your organization?

Fine-tuning your elevator pitch:

- To get started, brainstorm all that comes to your mind.
- Cut the jargon and details. Make short and powerful sentences, in conversational language. (Avoid slang, filler, words, and audible pauses.)
- Memorize the key points and practice <u>aloud.</u>
- Modify your elevator speech for the audience. (Are you delivering it to peers? Potential employers? An organization? Faculty members?)
- Start with an attention-getting opener: a single sentence that creates intrigue. Examples:

  (Liz) ...I want to help environmentalists spread the word about clean water.

  (Brett) ...I've always used my "left brain" to solve problems and that's why computer science is my passion.

  (Justin) ...I know a lot of people who could use a little help planning their financial future.

- Smile and show enthusiasm.
- Be brief. Be sincere.

REAL NETWORKING

"The currency of real networking is not greed but generosity."
—KEITH FERRAZZI

© VGstockstudio/Shutterstock.com

Social media aside, it's still people who matter in business. **People talking to people is how business gets done.**

The goal of networking should be to help people. Of course, you'd like them to help you out as well, especially when you're looking for an internship or job, but networking is a two-way street. If you remember that you should approach networking with the mindset of helping others, then asking for favors will be a lot easier one you've learned more about others and provided some value to them.

This short proverb is an excellent reminder of the importance of building a network:

> *If you want to be prosperous for a year, grow grain.*
> *If you want to prosperous for ten years, grow trees.*
> *If you want to be prosperous for a lifetime, grow people.*
> —PROVERB

Going Global

INTRODUCTION: BUSINESS ETIQUETTE ABROAD

The meaning of these words, said over two hundred years ago by Thomas Jefferson, is as important to doing business across cultures today as it was then. In his claim, Jefferson said that business has always prioritized profits, while patriotism, love of country, and the common good rank lower in concern. Showing respect for other cultures, especially when we are on "their turf," should be the mission of any businessperson who wants to have international doors opened to them.

John Breil, a man with a well-worn passport, had a thirty-year career in international business. As a member of our consulting team he tells our clients, "When going global – you have **A LOT** to learn, consider, and enjoy when doing business." (**A LOT** = Always Listen, Observe, and Think before you act.)

Even in your role as an intern or a new hire, chances are your company has a global presence. If they don't, companies they work with do. In our fully globalized times, today's entrepreneurs, regardless of their size, should become aware of international nuances and the protocols of doing business in other cultures.

You may be asked to help prepare your boss for an international trip, arrange a meeting for international partners or colleagues, or host an event with international guests. Don't take this task lightly. Just because you've had a Chinese roommate or a Peruvian professor doesn't mean that you're prepared to do business in these countries.

Think how you could use the following information to be more effective in the globally business-focused task you've been assigned as an intern or new hire:

BEST IN CLASS

Geography and government

- History, government structure, enemies/allies, currency, current issues
- Official language, official religion
- Climate, terrain, borders, neighbors, time zones

Logistics

- Passport/visa laws
- Traveling within the country, safety issues
- Communication vehicles, travel needs, health issues

Overview of communication and culture

- Collectivist vs. individualist
- Formal/informal, high/low context, direct/indirect communication, beliefs, role of relationships, role of gender, values and norms

Business practices

- Perception of time, greetings, handling business cards, titles, hierarchy, names and forms of address, gift giving, meeting protocol, technology, dress and appearance, language, expectations of management, intraoffice communication, work styles and habits, business-social events

Awareness of do's and taboos

- Business meals, tipping, toasts, verbal/nonverbal communication, family life, good luck/bad luck, meaning of colors, small talk

Listen, observe, and think

- Listen first, think second, speak third
- Be observant, be flexible, be patient, be respectful

THE CULTURAL ICEBERG

Many business associates I've met think that if they've been to a country two or three times, they know all of what they need to know about that culture to do business with them. They're wrong. They've only started their international business journey.

This photo illustrates some of the many aspects that make up a culture. Every culture has these, including our own. Easily observable actions and behaviors comprise only 10 to 15 percent of the cultural makeup. Like an iceberg, the vast majority of cultural norms are very subtle and hidden below the surface. It takes an investment of time—more than a few trips to that country—and patience to learn, understand, and appreciate what is below the water line. Without this investment, you can sink a global business relationship on its maiden voyage.

ACTIONS AND BEHAVIORS

HISTORY, GENDER, BELIEFS, MOTIVATION, CULTURAL CLIMATE, ASSUMPTIONS, CULTURE, EDUCATION, FOOD

A good place to start understanding different cultures is to identify the ways various cultures deliver messages. In his 1976 book *Beyond Culture*, anthropologist Edward Hall identified two distinct contexts: low-context and high-context cultures.

Low-context cultures use language primarily to express thoughts, feelings, and ideas. North American business practices tend to follow

low-context norms. Other examples include Germany, Norway, Denmark, Sweden, Switzerland, Finland, Canada, Australia, and Scandinavian countries.

High-context cultures rely on subtle, often nonverbal cues to convey meaning, save face, and maintain social harmony. How you speak, your nonverbal behaviors, and the history of your relationship will dictate the interaction you have with business associates in high-context cultures. Asian and South American business practices tend to follow high-context norms. Prime examples include Japan, China, Brazil, Mexico, Southern European countries, Arab countries, and African countries.

Similarly, **individualistic** cultures put their own interests and those of their family ahead of social concerns. Personal success is made possible through freedom to choose your own route to success. **Collectivistic** cultures have tight social frameworks in which members of an organization feel primary loyalty toward one another and the group. The belief is that the welfare of the organization is even *more important* than your own.

Here are some differences to consider:

Low-Context Cultures (Individualist)	High-Context Cultures (Collectivist)
Your goals are most important	The group's goals are most important
You're responsible for yourself	You're responsible for the entire group and their goals
Your success depends on surpassing others	Your success depends on your contribution
Competition is emphasized	Cooperation is emphasized and expected
Business is less formal	Business is more structured
Information is made explicit; little is left unsaid	Information is often implied or omitted from statements
Directness is valued; emails, texts, and online messaging are used to send quick and frequent messages	Indirectness is valued; longer forms of communication are used and basic questions are not always asked
Relationships last for a short amount of time or exist for a specific reason	Relationships are established before business transactions occur

No culture is completely high context, low context, individualist, or collectivist because all societies contain at least some parts that are both high and low. For example, while the United States is a low-context culture, family gatherings (which are common in our culture) tend to be high context.

The important thing to remember is that a little information goes a long way. In our training, we use a metaphor relating to understanding real estate to understanding cultures in business. Everyone knows the three most important words in real estate are: *location, location, location.* In doing business internationally, the three most important words to remember are:

- Patience—*in breaking through **language** barriers*
- Patience—*in breaking through **time and distance** barriers*
- Patience—*in breaking through **cultural** barriers*

ORGANIZATIONS ARE CULTURES, TOO

"To make customers happy, we have to make sure our employees are happy first."
—Tony Hsieh, Zappos

One of the important things for young professionals to consider is whether an organization is the right "cultural fit" for them. Whether in the United States or internationally, every organization has its own way of doing business, from the way people behave to the way they share information...all the way to how they celebrate success. You may hear employees at your internship or job site explain a process by saying, *"That's the way things are around here."* That's **organizational culture**.

Organizational culture can affect you in many ways. For example, *how long you work there, how cooperative or competitive coworkers will be, what kinds of fun are appropriate, how you're supposed to dress and behave, the amount of information you'll have access to*—organizational culture dictates all of these.

When you find the right "fit," your job will be satisfying. When you don't, it will be disappointing.

Look for answers to these questions:

- *Do the values of this organization match my values?*
- *Do I respect people in authority and consider them role models?*
- *Do I like the way people are treated in this environment?*
- *Am I comfortable with the way information is given?*
- *Am I comfortable with the way people communicate with each other? With superiors or subordinates?*
- *Am I comfortable with the way people are rewarded for their work?*
- *Do I see myself making a contribution and having an impact on this organization?*

While you're interning, you can make a lot of important observations that will clue you in to how you would "fit the culture" if you're hired. Conversations you have about the organization with other people who work there are key. How people communicate through email and at meetings is also important. Observe how people deal with paperwork, equipment, even office politics. Is the organization successful or teetering on the brink of failure?

When you first go to an organization for a face-to-face job interview, make a note of how you're treated before and after you arrive. Are people on time? Do prior emails and other forms of communication suggest an organized and welcoming culture? Are people smiling? Do they say "hello" or do they ignore you?

You're going to be spending a lot of time on the job. Think about the "personality" of that organization. Where you work will be just as important as where you live and who you spend your time with.

AVOIDING THE "UGLY AMERICAN" SYNDROME

by John R. Breil

> *"Traveling and change of place impart new vigor to the mind."*
> —SENECA, 4 B.C.

The term "Ugly American" was first used as the title of a photograph in 1948 of an American tourist in Havana. Since then, a book (1958) and a movie (1963) of the same name were introduced to the American public.

In a broad sense, the term refers to perceptions of loud, arrogant, demeaning, thoughtless, and self-centered behaviors of American citizens mainly abroad but also at home. In business, the term refers to boldness, brashness, and an unawareness of cultural nuances in business. In short, a lack of care and concern for others. Either way, the "Ugly American" syndrome is bad news for Americans doing business in other countries.

As American businesspeople, we have come a long way since 1963 in our willingness to learn to adapt to other cultures, but there's still much more work to do and today, even more at stake. As a student, take advantage of all opportunities to travel and study abroad. It will be an asset to your career and of high interest to a hiring manager of a company with global presence. If you can speak another language or have lived in another county, it's a huge plus.

It pays to think about the impression you make to avoid the "Ugly American" syndrome."

Respect the Position or Hierarchy

Americans tend to be more informal. CEOs, directors, managers, and business leaders are complimented when their subordinates describe them as "just like the rest of us." In most cases, first names are used regardless of position or responsibility. In most other countries, business is more hierarchical and aimed at creating a culture of respect and stability. More formality is followed, and the use of last names and titles is expected. For example, disagreeing with a superior in a Japanese business culture is considered highly disrespectful. Know your international counterparts (even as an intern or new hire) and be prepared to adjust and find ways you can help your bosses adjust.

Raise Your Cultural Awareness

Remember the acronym **G-L-O-B-A-L** we shared earlier in this chapter, with a breakdown of how you can prepare for international business meetings and events with international colleagues and clients. Interacting with another culture in another part of the world requires preparation. Read as much as you can about the other culture or country and their business environment and learn about the people you'll be interacting with. And don't forget the other acronym **A L-O-T**; you have **A LOT** to learn when doing business internationally: Always Listen, Observe, Think.

Make a Good First Impression

Learn the names and titles of your international guests or hosts. Know the responsibilities of the persons you'll be meeting with in advance, so you don't embarrass yourself at a meeting. Get pronunciations ahead of time, if possible. It's okay to ask the person you're meeting to help you say his or her name correctly. Remember, to be safe, always use Mr. or Miss unless you are totally certain the woman is married, in which case you could use Ms. or Mrs. Official titles (Dr., Atty, Judge, Mayor) are important and should be used whenever appropriate.

Learn a few words or phrases in other languages and know how to pronounce them *correctly*. A "hello" or "thank you" in the language of your global partners goes a long way to showing your cultural sensitivity and flexibility. A bonus is if you have someone in your organization who speaks their language and could be included in a first meeting.

Follow the local customs of that culture when you're a guest and you're being introduced. In some cultures, you hug, in others you kiss, and in others you shake hands.

The handshake is internationally accepted for business, though some cultures may not be comfortable with touching due to deeply rooted religious or cultural customs. A pharmaceutical client of ours was sensitive to this phenomenon when sending their sales reps to doctor's offices. In their case, female sales reps knew *not* to initiate a handshake with male Jewish doctors who practiced conservative religious rules.

When you're hosting international guests at your company's location in the United States, expect that you'll be shaking hands. In the United States, we judge people's personality and their confidence level based on the way they shake hands. That's not true for other cultures. Here are some differences:

- In Europe: Firm grip; two to three pumps. Light kisses (two or three on alternating cheeks) *may* be exchanged after a relationship develops.
- Asia: Lighter grip (may include a slight bow); ten to twelve seconds for entire interaction.
- Middle East: Lighter grasp; two to three pumps; hand may be held for longer time after shaking; no extended eye contact; no two-handed handshakes. (Two-handed handshakes should be avoided in all international settings.)

WATCH YOUR BODY LANGUAGE

Many times, we fail to do our homework when it comes to body language in international business, and the wrong move can be a surefire way to get on the nerves of your international counterparts before a relationship even has a chance to develop.

Understand the concept of "personal space." We might feel uncomfortable when someone stands less than two feet from us. Roger Axtell, author of eight international etiquette guides, including *Do's and Taboos Around the World*, says that Latin America and the Middle East have smaller personal space "bubbles" (one foot or less) so you should refrain from stepping away when they move close to you.

Hand gestures and facial expressions also do not translate similarly in all cultures. A "thumbs up," the "OK" sign, the "V" sign, pointing something out with a finger, or even a wave could mean something different or even be offensive in another country. Open-handed gestures, with all fingers generally together, is usually considered the safest approach.

Recently, I traveled to Bulgaria and learned that nodding your head "yes" means "no," whereas shaking your head "no" means "yes." This reminded me of one of my early trips to Japan. I gave a sales presentation to a group of Japanese clients. Fortunately, their understanding of English was sufficient for me to speak without needing an interpreter.

During my presentation they seemed to be paying attention and many times nodded their heads when I made key points. I left this meeting feeling very positive and thinking I had support for my proposals. During the train ride back to our Tokyo office, I commented to our Japanese sales manager that the clients liked my presentation and agreed to move forward. He paused, looked at me with an astonished scowl on his face, and explained that the nodding did NOT mean agreement, understanding, or acceptance. It did NOT even mean that they understood the words I was speaking. It only meant that they could hear the sound of my voice in their ears! He paused and said, "Breil-san, you have a lot to learn about doing business in Japan."

USE CLEAR ENGLISH

Speak at a slower pace (not louder) when you're with those who do not speak English fluently. My practice is to always speak at 75 percent of the pace I would speak when I am at home or in my U.S. office. Avoid irritating phrases that include heavy use of acronyms, slang, and jargon.

Idioms, which are words and phrases akin to the people of a country, are not easily understood, so avoid these business idioms: *cut to the chase, going postal, hit it out of the park.* Non-English speakers can also struggle to interpret vagueness, so avoid phrases like, *"I'm not sure"* or *"I can't say."* Instead of asking, *"Do you understand?"* ask *"Am I making myself clear?"* Most of all, apologize for not speaking their language and thank them for their willingness to communicate in English.

The use of double negatives can be very confusing. For example, replying *"Not too bad"* when asked how you are.

DON'T MAKE CARELESS JUDGMENTS

Seemingly innocent observations that compare how their country is different from your home can come across as superior or rude, so be careful. Examples include, *"I can't believe this restaurant doesn't have ice cubes"* or *"Your currency is funny-looking; sort of like play money"* or *"We would never do it that way!"*

BE A CONSIDERATE HOST AND GUEST

Small gifts to your hosts when traveling internationally or when they arrive in the United States as your guests don't have to be expensive, but they must have quality and perceived value.

Here are some guidelines to use if you're tasked with getting gifts for international guests or colleagues you or your counterparts will be doing business with.

Country/ Location	Appropriate Gifts	Occasion
Eastern or Western Europe	▪ Quality logo items from your company ▪ Books that represent a sport or hobby of the recipient	Large groups: the top person Small groups: each person
Asia	▪ Liquor (Korea, China) ▪ Leather items ▪ Baseball caps and t-shirts from well-known teams	To celebrate an agreement or present upon guest's arrival in U.S.
Central and South America	▪ Gifts of value or importance (no trinkets) ▪ Leather items	Present at social functions, not business meetings
India and Middle East	▪ Quality logo items from your company ▪ Toys made in the U.S. if they have children	Present at end of business meetings
Appropriate for mostly all countries/ cultures	▪ Items from your state or region (nonperishable foods, crafts, small décor items) ▪ Books with U.S./regional landscapes ▪ Quality pen and pencil sets ▪ Something you've created yourself; a craft, painting, photograph	Present at beginning or end of business meetings

Always take time to think about the gift you are giving and the recipient. Gifts are given to build the relationship and sometimes when you clinch the deal. How the gift is wrapped is as important as what is inside, so do research on how to wrap and present your gift. (A plastic pen with your company's logo is *never* an appropriate gift...anywhere.)

TEN COMMANDMENTS FOR GOING GLOBAL

by John R. Breil

> *"Travel is fatal to prejudice, bigotry and narrow-mindedness."*
> —MARK TWAIN, 1835-1910

© 24Novembers/Shutterstock.com

1. **Know the difference between collectivist and individualist cultures.**
   You're already familiar with this concept from our explanation at the beginning of this chapter. Another way to look at the cultural climate is to consider the *physical* climate. It seems simple

enough, but there's some merit to considering that warmer climate countries tend to be more collectivistic (high-context) cultures and colder climate countries tend to be more individualistic (low-context) cultures. In theory, cultural norms in warmer climate countries value feelings and emotions. While people in warmer climate countries are open to discuss and consider new ideas, they value harmony and consensus within the group. Warm climate cultures also take a longer time to make decisions.

Cold climate cultures are more direct. People in colder climate countries want to deal with facts and proven data. Emotions and feelings are less important, and decisions are made more quickly.

2. **Understand the interpretation of time.**
   It can be a culture shock to learn how people from other cultures understand and use time. One year, I gave my wife a watch with two faces so that when we travel she can set one to the zone of where we are and one to the zone of home. North Americans and most northern Europeans have a **monochronic** view of time. To these cultures, time is *money*. You'll hear people talk about *saving time, making time, having time, wasting time, using time,* and *taking time*. Time is carefully rationed. Appointments are scheduled and adhered to.

   Conversely, Latin American, Middle Eastern, and southern European cultures have a **polychronic** view of time. Time is more fluid. Meetings can go on for as long as it takes to decide or reach agreement (I've been there!). Meetings don't end just because "it's time." Members of these cultures are less concerned with punctuality and more concerned with relational factors. Being "on time" takes on a whole different meaning, and varying degrees of lateness are acceptable. My experience is that meetings in Europe typically begin on time, meetings in Asia start and end on time, and meetings in South America are less structured with a more fluid start time and end time.

3. **Dress the part.**
   Business casual has become the "norm" in the United States, but it is not so in most other countries. Dress in conservative "global colors" (grays, blues, blacks). Avoid distracting colors and patterns. Men should wear a suit or sport coat and tie for first-time business meetings; women should wear a conservative dress or

pantsuit. Pack conservatively if you're visiting warm climate cultures, even though the temperature might be more appropriate for shorts, t-shirts, and sandals.

One of my direct reports arrived at the hotel after a long flight from Washington, D.C. to Tokyo. I told him we would meet in the lobby and go straight to the meeting after he checked into his room and changed. He arrived in the lobby with the same clothes he wore to travel. We were on a tight schedule, but I insisted he change into more appropriate clothes for our business meeting with our colleagues from the Japanese office.

On the way to the meeting, I explained that there's no such thing as business casual in Japan and for him to dress too casually would send a message to our counterparts the meeting is not important to us. An appearance that is too casual also places doubt about your skills and knowledge. It's the perfect example of the phrase "judging a book by its cover"!

4. **Know the protocol of greetings and "power distance."**
Business exchanges are more formal, especially at the beginning of a relationship. It's important to learn names and titles (the use of titles is important). Use last names until you're invited to address the person by his or her first name.

Some examples are:

Germany = "Herr" or "Frau" for Mr./Ms.

France = "Monsieur" or "Madame" for Mr./Ms.

Japan = "san" is added to the last (*not* first) name for both genders; example: Breil "san"

The term **power distance** is important in international business and refers to attitudes toward differences in authority. For example, cultures with a **high power distance** (Mexico, Philippines) accept the fact that power is distributed unequally and that some people have access to greater resources and thus more influence than others. Differences in status and rank are routine and expected, and employees in high positions are respected. **Low power distance** cultures like the United States downplay differences in power. Employees will challenge their leaders and may expect to gain greater influence by doing so.

* As a young professional in the United States, you should be aware of and show respect for those in power, but also voice your opinion when you have something important to say. But beware, don't be overly aggressive in challenging your superiors until you've gained some experience and credibility, or you could be viewed as overly aggressive.

5. **Know the nuances of business card exchange.**
   A proper business card exchange is very important in Asian business cultures, it's a ritual. Here are some rules for exchanging cards:
   - Have your cards available always.
   - Keep your cards in a nice case; no creases, dirt, or pen marks.
   - Men, keep cards in your front inside jacket pocket; women, keep cards in your purse, a pocket, or brief case, easily accessible.
   - Present your card with the written information facing the recipient. (In Japanese cultures, present your card with two hands.)
   - Accept the other's card and study it. (In Japanese cultures a slight bow might accompany the exchange; accept the card with two hands and study it, noting family name and given name and how they are listed on the card. A Japanese businessperson will be introduced to you by his or her "family" name.)
   - Keep the card out and on the table if you're in a meeting and arrange them in the same order as people are seated.
   - Do not write on someone else's card or deface it in any way while you are with them. Later, make notes on the cards of the date and location of the meeting. Underline the family name for future reference.

6. **Participate in after-hours social events.**
   Social events are important to building relationships with international colleagues and clients. Several years ago, on a trip to Asia, we finished a meeting and I invited our international colleagues to join me for dinner. They politely refused. I figured they wanted to return to their homes for the evening. The next morn-

ing, I learned from an insider that my colleagues were offended I had asked only once and accepted their first answer as final. Had I asked a second time, they were ready to accept. Refusing after the first invitation, then accepting after a second, was the way their culture treated a business social invitation. I had the right idea, but the wrong approach.

In the United States, business transactions occur, and relationships follow. In most other countries, relationships are first established, then business follows. I've attended many dinners and receptions with "jet lag," but I powered my way through them all because I knew it was a golden opportunity to start a relationship with my international colleagues and clients, and it would pave the way to doing business with them in the future.

Do participate in after-hours events. Don't use this time to focus on business, though; rather, use this time to sell yourself and improve communication and breakdown cultural barriers. Find out what you have in common with your international business colleagues and focus on these points to make a stronger, more lasting, and favorable impression.

7. **Know how and when to engage in small talk.**
    There's a powerful story illustrating the dynamics of approaching strangers and engaging in small talk. Years ago, Walmart opened stores in Germany. They wanted to carry over their personal "folksy approach," so they made certain to have greeters at the doors, smiling and welcoming shoppers. The Germans, with their more formal attitude, were offended by this casual approach from strangers. The German shopper was there to buy products, not make friends. This led to other cultural and economic clashes, and after nine years Walmart sold all their stores to a German competitor and walked away from a $400 billion retail market!

    Because business relationships are established in many otherwise "social" situations, there are plenty of opportunities to engage in conversation with your international business colleagues. "Small talk" is not idle banter, as some business experts claim. It is a way to engage with others and build relationships no matter *where* you're doing business.

    Polite conversation with international business colleagues is expected and welcome, but you should know what topics are acceptable and what topics are unacceptable and which are not so you don't embarrass others or yourself. Here's a guide to safe topics and topics to avoid:

SAFE TOPICS	TOPICS TO AVOID
Weather	Politics (especially a war where they were *not* allies)
Your flight to their locale	
Where you're from in the U.S.	Religion
	Work ethics
Noncontroversial current events or world news	
	Controversial subjects (political issues; topics relating to sex or sexual habits)
Travel and tourism	
Hobbies	Cost of items
International sports (not those exclusive to Americans)	Poverty in their country
	Personal issues or misfortunes
Cultural events (art, music, theatre)	
	Jokes/stories of questionable taste
Food/dining (beer discussions in Germany; sake discussions in Japan)	
	Your health/other's health
Work (company history; special projects)	Bad mouthing the competition
History	Social issues
Culture and tradition	Children/family (in early stages of meeting international colleagues it's perceived as too personal)
Automobiles and transportation innovations	
Local events in their home country/city	

8. **Format emails with clarity and a personal touch.**
    International business emails are more formal than in the United States. Here are some e-communication tips:
    *   Always include a proper greeting.
    *   Keep communication more formal at the start of a relationship.
    *   Start with a non-business comment, for example - "*I hope you're enjoying good weather*" or "*I hope you're having a good day*"

- Be clear about actions to be taken.
- When referencing a date, spell out the month (July 11, 2018, not 7/11/18; in many countries this is Nov. 7, 2018).
- Be specific about times (*"I will call you at **11 AM** or **1100** hours your time in Tokyo"*).
- Learn a few words or phrases in their language (*Guten Tag, Herr Klotz*).
- Keep sentences short and concise. (Remember, your international business colleagues are doing *you* a favor using English.)

Here's a sample email to international business associates:

To: John Smith, Hans van Egmond, Amy Chan, Claude Mercer, Hilde Werner, Fumi Kurahaski, Clayton Robbins

cc: Tom Aggers, V.P of Operations

Subject: Budget Revisions for Upcoming Sales meeting in October

Greetings to everyone. I look forward to meeting all of you at our annual sales meeting 26-30 of October, in Hamburg Germany.

Please bring your revised operating budgets to this meeting. The budgets will be discussed the first full day of the meeting, 27 October (Tuesday). The specifications from Tom Aggers, V.P. of Operations, are attached in this email.

Our meeting will start at 0830 in the main conference room in the Steigenberger Hotel, where you will be staying.

Please let me know if I can help with any additional logistics for this meeting.

Thank you,

John

John Breil, *Administrative Intern for Tom Aggers*
The Professional Edge, Inc.
York PA 17604
Email: john@theprofessionaledgeinc.com
Phone: 800-555-1234

9. Know local dining customs in advance.

"They say you have to stop eating when he does.
But what if he's having a snack and you're starving?
Do you have to eat fast?"
—CHARLES BARKLEY, U.S. PRO BASKETBALL STAR
(REFERRING TO MONACO'S PRINCE RAINIER)

© Evgeny Litvinov/Shutterstock.com

Hamburger mentalities need not apply. Be prepared to try local foods and save your negative commentary for when you return home. An unwillingness to try local foods could be to your peril in international dining situations.

On my very first trip to Asia in 1986, I accompanied our group vice president. Our first stop was Tokyo. We met with a Japanese company that had distributed our products for many years. We were taken to lunch at a formal Japanese restaurant, complete with tatami mats and servers dressed in silk kimonos. We were escorted to the table in a private room. I knew enough to remove my shoes before entering, then I took a seat on the floor facing the entrance to the room. Throughout the meal, the servers approached me before the others and showed me the dish which was to be served to the entire group. I wasn't sure what to do, but I gave a polite nod. After we had left our hosts, I asked our VP why the servers came to me first. He told me that I had taken the seat reserved for "the most important person from our team," which was him. I apologized to him and asked why he didn't ask me to change my seat at the start of the lunch. He said, "I knew our hosts well enough to let you go ahead and make a fool of yourself. Besides, what better way for you to learn an important lesson."

This was an important lesson learned. Seating protocol is important in international meetings and dining settings, especially in Asian business cultures. If you're planning a dining event for a group your organization will host, be proactive and plan the seating in advance. Let everyone on your team know ahead of time so that they are aware of the seating arrangements.

Other dining customs to consider if you're the host are dietary restrictions (many Indian cultures are vegetarian or vegan, and Middle Eastern cultures do not eat pork, for example). Religious limitations could also dictate whether or not alcohol is offered.

If you're the guest, be willing to try the local foods and don't complain about the food or service. Rather, take full advantage of the opportunity to build relationships!

10. **Speak the language.**
English is the international language of business but that doesn't mean you shouldn't make an effort to learn and use a few phrases in the language of the country you're visiting or hosting. Common phrases are good *morning/afternoon/evening, please/thank you, good day, yes/no.*

On the other hand, don't pretend you know how to speak the language when you don't. For example, ordering your meal in French at a French restaurant only works when you can sound authentic, not arrogant.

Language and communication in international business:

1. General guidelines for speaking
   • Use short, concise sentences.
   • Use pauses frequently.

- Do not use jargon, slang, or regional expressions.
- Do not use double negatives *(Example: "We don't need no interpreter" or "I'm not too bad").*
- Use standard terminology (e.g., do not use synonyms).
- Be cautious with humor; it does not always translate.
- Be aware of the value of silence.
- Do not let yourself be affected or concerned with the relatively high emotional tone that may accompany business discussions.

2. When English is the second language
- Speak at a measured pace; do not speak more loudly.
- Understand and speak in "international English, not American English."
- Apologize for <u>your</u> accent.
- Thank them for conducting the meeting in English.

3. Using an interpreter
- Use a professional interpreter. Make sure he or she understands your business.
- Privately review with the interpreter the "spirit" of what you are trying to communicate, rather than the literal translation.

- Be prepared to speak at half-pace with frequent pauses.
- Put your information into "chunks" with frequent breaks. Have the interpreter field comments and questions to you so you can check understanding.
- Speak directly to and make eye contact with the individual or group. Do not look at the interpreter.

4. Listening to international English
- Repeat what you believe was said. Ask for verification.
- Ask questions to clarify and confirm understanding on both sides. Also, many cultures expect verbal "prompts" to show that you are listening. (Example: *"Thank you, I agree. Please continue."*)
- Mirror their level of eye contact and body language.
- Take notes. If possible, have someone from your group take notes when you're speaking.

Participating in international business meetings:
- Remain seated during a meeting unless you are getting up to write on a board or illustrate a point.
- Raise your voice slightly or use a *controlled* form of anger (with discretion) to emphasize key points or as a negotiating tactic.
- Stay focused, interested, and involved in the group during a business meeting.
- Do not point at an individual during a business presentation.
- Many English technical or business terms are carried over to other languages. When another language is being spoken, listen for English words and terminology (some words are the same in many languages) to gain some idea of what is being discussed.
- Take notes while another person from your group is speaking or controlling the meeting.
- Do not play with objects (e.g., pencils or pens), fidget, or doodle during a business meeting as it conveys a lack of interest.
- Do not verbally single out an individual when discussing sensitive topics.
- Watch your body language to appear interested and involved.

ARE YOU UP FOR THE GLOBAL CHALLENGE?

> *"To ensure continuing prosperity in the global economy, nothing is more important than the development and application of knowledge and skills."*
>
> —MARTIN REES

Crossing cultures can be challenging, frustrating, and time consuming. It can also be very rewarding when you find the common ground to move an idea forward or a business deal to a successful conclusion.

It can also be a valuable way for you to gain visibility and advance more quickly in most organizations, if you're up to the challenge.

Remember to have *patience* because you have **A LOT** to learn, and also **A LOT** to gain when "going global"!